Essential Skills for a Brilliant Family Dog

Books 1-4

Beverley Courtney

Copyright © 2016 Beverley Courtney

The right of Beverley Courtney to be identified as the author of the work has been asserted by her in accordance with the Copyright, Designs and Patents Act 1988.

All rights reserved. No part of this publication may be reproduced or transmitted in any form or by any means, electronic or otherwise, without written permission from the author.

www.brilliantfamilydog.com

Books by the author

Essential Skills for a Brilliant Family Dog

Book 1 Calm Down! *Step-by-Step to a Calm, Relaxed, and Brilliant Family Dog*

Book 2 Leave It! *How to teach Amazing Impulse Control to your Brilliant Family Dog*

Book 3 Let's Go! *Enjoy Companionable Walks with your Brilliant Family Dog*

Book 4 Here Boy! *Step-by-step to a Stunning Recall from your Brilliant Family Dog*

Essential Skills for your *Growly* but Brilliant Family Dog

Book 1 Why is my Dog so Growly? *Teach your fearful, aggressive, or reactive dog confidence through understanding*

Book 2 Change for your Growly Dog! *Action steps to build confidence in your fearful, aggressive, or reactive dog*

Book 3 Calm walks with your Growly Dog *Strategies and techniques for your fearful, aggressive, or reactive dog*

www.brilliantfamilydog.com/books

Free Training for you!

Jumping up?

Barking?

Chewing?

Get inventive solutions to everyday problems with your dog

www.brilliantfamilydog.com

Disclaimer

I have made every effort to make my teachings crystal clear, but we're dealing with live animals here (That's you, and your dog.) and I can't see whether you're doing it exactly right. I am unable to guarantee success, as it depends entirely on the person utilising the training programs, strategies, tools, and resources.

What I do know is that this system works!

Nothing in these books should upset or worry your dog in any way, but if your dog has a pre-existing problem of fear or aggression you should consult a force-free trainer to help. www.brilliantfamilydog.com/growly will get you started.

By the way, to simplify matters I refer to our trainee dog throughout this series as "she." "He" and "she" will both learn the exact same way. The cumbersome alternatives of "he/she" or "they" depersonalise our learner: I want her to be very real to you!

All the photos in this book are of "real" dogs – either my own, or those of students and readers (with their permission). So the reproduction quality is sometimes not the best. I have chosen the images carefully to illustrate the concepts – so we'll have to put up with some fuzziness.

Contents

Book 1 - Calm Down! 1

Introduction Time for a change 3
    Just one skill is needed 7
    Dogs are doers 8

Chapter 1 Introducing the Mat! 9
    What do you need? 10
    Your Mat 10
    Treats 10
    Troubleshooting 12

Chapter 2 Starting with the Mat 13
    Lesson 1 Front paws on the Mat 14
    Troubleshooting 16

Chapter 3 Mat Magic! 21
    Lesson 2 Down on the Mat 22
    How do I get my dog to lie down? 23
    Troubleshooting 25
    Lesson 3 Learning when to get off the mat 26
    Troubleshooting 28

Chapter 4 What do I do with this mat now? 31
    Coffee with a friend, or Sunday lunch at the pub 32
    A peaceful evening in the living room 33
    Visiting the vet 35
    Family picnic 37

Chapter 5 Taking it on the road 39
    The doorbell! 40
    Targets 41
    Preparing dinner 43
    Mat substitutes 43
    Reports from the Front Line 44

Chapter 6 Surprise benefits of Mat Magic! 47
    How should our day go? 49

Conclusion 51
    This is just the beginning for you! 51

Resources 53

Book 2 - Leave It! 55

Introduction Now you see it, now you don't 57

Chapter 1 It's all about choice 61
    Choices, choices 63
    Special equipment you'll need to teach Impulse Control 64
    How to reward your dog for her brilliant self-control 65

Chapter 2 Introducing the Magic Hand 69
    Lesson 1 Teaching the Magic Hand Game 70
    Troubleshooting 72
    How will this help with everyday grabbing and stealing? 74
    Life becomes simpler 75

Chapter 3 Keeping away from dropped or found food on the ground 77
    Lesson 2 Teaching the Food-on-the-Floor Game, or Magic Hand 2.0 80
    Troubleshooting 81
    Lesson 3 Bringing the game to real life! 82
    An important word about words 84
    Lesson 4 Adding the cue 85

Troubleshooting 85
Lacy's Find 86

Chapter 4 Why does it work?.. 87
People first... 87
Pavlov's Dogs and Classical Conditioning 88
How does this apply to us?... 89
Operant Conditioning.. 90
Why does this matter to me and my pet dog? 91
A word about punishment 92

Chapter 5 Here comes the joy!.. 95
1. The Door 95
2. The Car Door... 96
3. The Crate 98
4. Furniture 99
5. Toy Play 100
6. Reclaiming Stolen Shoes.. 101
7. Mugging Your Hand or Your Pocket for Those Treats 102
8. Tasty Shopping Bags in the Car... 103
9. Helping Tidy Up the Kitchen (aka Countersurfing) 104
10. Marking Every Tree... 104
11. Passing Quietly By Previously Exciting Things 105
12. Meet and Greet Nicely 105
The Premack Principle 106

Chapter 6 The effect of Impulse Control on the two of you................ 109
What effect will this have on my dog?... 109
So how will all this affect me? 111
Mutual trust 111
Side effects... 112
That's mine! 114
It's all tricks to them 116
Food on The Paws 116
Troubleshooting 117

Food on the Head 117
    The Famous Tossing the Biscuit off the Nose Trick 118

Conclusion You are a huge way into your journey! 121

Resources 123
    Works consulted for Chapter 4 124

Book 3 - Let's Go! 127

Introduction Oh no! Not again! 129

Chapter 1 Equipment that will help you…and equipment to avoid like the plague 133
    So if it's so bad, why on earth do dogs do it? 134
    But my dog is big and strong! 135
    Collars 135
    The Collar Hold 136
    Harness 137
    Head Halters 138
    Leads 139
    Devices used by the Inquisition 140
    What's a clicker and do I have to use one? 141
    Treats 142
    Troubleshooting 143

Chapter 2 Change your mindset first 145
    Holding the lead 146
    You never have to pull your dog's lead again! 147
    Key Lead Skill No.1 Holding the Lead 147
    What you accept is what you get 148
    Time to keep still 149
    Key Lead Skill No.2 Parking 149
    Troubleshooting 150

Chapter 3 If she's not out front, where should she be? 153
    Lesson 1: Teaching your dog to find the Reward Spot 154
    Watchpoints.. 155
    Your first tentative steps... 157
    Lesson 2: Reward Spot on the Move... 158
    Troubleshooting 159

Chapter 4 Keeping those hands soft at all times 163
    You really never have to pull your dog's lead again!...................... 164
    Key Lead Skill No. 3 Slow Stop 164
    Troubleshooting 165
    You really, really, never have to pull your dog's lead again!............ 166
    Key Lead Skill No. 4 Lead Stroking... 167
    Troubleshooting 168
    The very beginnings of your companionable walk....................... 169
    Troubleshooting 169

Chapter 5 Get moving! 173
    1 2 3 Treat!... 173
    Lesson 3: Checking in... 174
    Troubleshooting 174
    Let's take this on the road 177
    More advanced stuff 178
    Really advanced stuff 178
    Lesson 4: Moving past distractions.. 179

Chapter 6 Complications? 181
    "My dog's friendly!" 182

Conclusion A new life ahead of us 185
    Spin-offs 185
    Top up the learning.. 186

Resources... 187
    Harness 188
    For Challenging Dogs... 188

Book 4 - Here Boy!..191

Introduction...193

Chapter 1 What you need to have and know to get success.............199
   Treats: what and why? 200
   Control the rewards and you control the dog.................................202
   What the stylish well-behaved dog is wearing 204
   Collar 205
   Harness 205
   Lead 206

Chapter 2 What is a recall? 209
   Your brand new puppy...210
   Call just once...210
   Name versus sound..211
   ACTION STEP Making your dog's name wonderful.....................212
   Speed, joy, and enthusiasm..212
   Follow through..213
   Puppy vs. mature dog vs. new rescue dog..................................213
   Pavlov (not the creamy meringue dessert, but the scientist)............214
   Dogs do what works..215
   9 Rules for the Perfect Recall 215

Chapter 3 Now the fun starts! 217
   Learning to pay attention 218
   Lesson 1: The Focus Game..219
   Lesson 2: The Name Game 219
   Troubleshooting..220
   Taking the Name Game on the road 224
   Troubleshooting..226

Chapter 4 Four more classic recall games.................................229
   Lesson 3: The Running Name Game.......................................230
   Troubleshooting..230
   Lesson 4: Puppy Pingpong 232

Troubleshooting 233
Lesson 5: Cannonball Recall 235
Troubleshooting 237
Lesson 6: Torpedo Recall... 238
Troubleshooting 240
Distractions and Distance 242

Chapter 5 Taking it outside - rabbits and other beasts 245
Those squirrels!... 246

Conclusion The end of this road - but the beginning of your journey . 249
Recalls and related things 249

Resources 253
Works consulted for Chapter 2 254
Harness 254

Appreciation 255

About the author 257

Essential Skills for a Brilliant Family Dog

Book 1
Calm Down!

Step-by-Step to a Calm, Relaxed, and Brilliant Family Dog

Beverley Courtney

Introduction
Time for a change

Coco (15 weeks) says, "If this thing is on the ground, I must need to sit on it."

You, your dog and your family have had a great outing, seeing the sights of the seaside town - the beach, the castle, the ramparts, the quaint streets, and the shops. You all are now exhausted and need to stop for coffee and cakes, fizz and crisps - the perfect finish to a family day out. But your dog is having none of it! You'd think she'd be worn out by now with all that tramping along cobbled streets, the run on the beach, splashing in the waves, clambering up stone steps, rolling in that dead fish …

Possibly it's because she's tired that she's being so difficult now. She won't settle - she's poking and pestering at hands and elbows, jogging your arm so your coffee sploshes on your lap. She's whining and pacing. She's begging for food. She doesn't seem to know how to switch off.

Does this picture look familiar? What can you do about this other than nagging, tutting, and keeping her on a tight lead?

There's a secret that a lot of family dog owners just don't know - and I'm going to explain its mysteries to you here.

We all seek security and a place to belong, a place where we can relax and feel at ease. As soon as we're in a strange place again, we get anxious and fidgety. Witness how long it takes people to choose a table in even an almost empty cafe!

A fretful toddler can halt her tears and become calm just by clutching her security blanket or beloved teddy bear close to her. Your dog is just the same. She needs to feel secure and safe in order to settle. She also needs to know that settling down is all she has to do right now.

Just before we start, let's have a look at some of the situations where this technique I'm going to teach you can help. Do they resonate with you? Does your dog do any of these things? One or two of them may be major annoyances for you. There may be others that are minor irritations that you didn't even know could be fixed!

- You've managed to infiltrate a visitor into your house and your dog will not leave them alone! Now your guest is giving you a stiff smile from behind a flurry of paws and tail, assuring you they don't mind - all the time wishing they hadn't come.
- You want to settle down for a picnic during a day out and your dog is trampling over the blanket, treading in the food, stealing the

sandwiches … You can't relax and enjoy some quiet time with your family.

- You open the car door and your dog comes flying out to play an infuriating chase game around the car, leap up at a passing pensioner, or - tragically - run into the road.

- You're trying to help the children get their homework done while also organising their meal, but your dog continually interrupts proceedings by trying to steal the food you're making and disturbing the children. You've tried putting her in the garden, but she just barks and digs up the flowerbeds.

- You've had a nice family walk with your dog. You need to get everyone loaded back in the car with all their toys, bikes, and stuff. Your dog decides to play a game of Keep Away. She won't come to have her feet dried and get into the car.

- You're at the vets and your dog is straining on the lead, trying to get at the cat in its basket, jumping up at anyone who walks past, making you feel quite inadequate at being able to control her.

- Your dog never stops. She goes on and on and on. She doesn't rest - in fact, she seems to get more frantic, busy, and difficult as the day goes on. She totally resists the vital restorative sleep you know she needs.

- You find yourself thinking, "Whose idea was it to get a dog?"

Recognise any of these? They are all common events in many homes, and they really add up to a lot of frustration and annoyance. You chose to get a family dog because of the pleasure and richness she'd bring to your lives, but when your dog is driving you mad on a daily basis, you wonder how it's gone so wrong. That pleasure and richness can feel so far away.

It was having to learn the techniques to make a Brilliant Family Dog with my own busy household of multiple dogs, cats, sheep, goats, hens, and children that set me on the road to helping others do the same. I learnt early on that forcing someone to do something only resulted in grudging compliance at best; whereas getting them to participate and enjoy the process turned them into eager and fast learners. This applied equally to the dogs, the goats - and the children! The sheep and the cats not so much.

My qualifications range from the understanding of learning theory to specialist work for fearful, anxious, and growly dogs. Acquiring an anxious, growly dog of my own ensured that I learnt and understood the process of assimilating the dog into our world in a way which built her confidence.

There are some superb teachers and advocates of force-free dog training, and you'll find those I am particularly indebted to in the Resources section at the end of this book. Some of the methods I'll be showing you are well-known in the force-free dog training community, while many have my own particular twist.

My work revolves around puppies, new rescue dogs, growly dogs - and, of course, dog owners! There are many people more gifted than I who can train animals to do astonishing things. My gift lies in being able to convey my knowledge to the dog's caregiver in a way which has them saying, "It's so obvious when you put it like that!"

Dogs are individuals and so are their owners, so sometimes creativity and imagination are needed to solve a problem. There isn't a one-size-fits-all approach to training - as you'll see when you look at the Troubleshooting sections following each lesson in the book.

Here are some tips to keep in mind as you go through this book:

- Keep sessions very, very short - ten treats may be plenty long enough
- Keep treats flowing very fast whenever you're teaching anything new
- Remember that frustration and annoyance will not help anyone, so if things aren't going well in your (very short) session, just call it a day, have a game with your dog, and try again later.
- Move your training to different locations as you build up your dog's love of this game. First of all, just a different room in the house.

If you focus on this as a project - having just one short session a day - you'll be amazed how quickly you reach the stage of being able to use your new skills anywhere, any time.

Follow the steps that I outline for you. Don't skip or jump ahead. Work on each step till it's more or less right, then move on. There's no need to be a perfectionist here. You don't want to get stuck.

I suggest you read the whole book before you start so you yourself are clear about what you need and what you are aiming for. Then re-read the lesson you're working on and go straight into your very short session. After this you can assess where you are and check the Troubleshooting section for any difficulties that are relevant to you and your dog. Then you'll be ready for your next session the next day.

Just one skill is needed

You may be surprised to learn that all the pictures I painted before (and many more) can be completely resolved by one simple technique. You teach your dog to LOVE her mat - her security blanket - a place to find comfort and freedom from anxiety. Once she does, she will become putty in your hands.

And no! It's not difficult to teach. Even young puppies in an exciting environment can learn this invaluable skill quickly.

Puppies from 16-20 weeks resting quietly on their mats before Puppy Class begins

Dogs are doers

They can't exist in a vacuum. They need to be doing something. Teaching your dog to keep her mat on the floor by lying on top of it is the perfect solution to relieving anxiety and stress.

All you need is a small mat and a bit of teaching to make your dog feel secure and at home, even when she's out. She'll have a place she can rest and relax without worrying about where she is or what she should be doing.

In this book, I'll show you how to get your dog manic about her mat. As soon as you put it down she will hurl herself onto it as if it might float away and escape if she's not fast enough! She will stay firmly on her mat, anchoring it to the floor, and she will even stay there regardless of how many crumbs the children drop, until you are ready to release her.

The magical aspects of the mat are that it:

- Acts like a toddler's security blanket, making your dog feel comfortable and at ease
- Creates a bubble for the dog to stay in safely while she observes the world, dispelling the anxiety she might otherwise feel
- Builds a state of relaxation which becomes connected with the mat; i.e. dog on mat = snoozing dog
- Is especially valuable with reactive or anxious dogs; they don't have to be on guard duty the whole time
- Keeps your dog content and amused when coupled with treats or a food-toy
- Your dog thinks, "I know what I should be doing," as she settles down

Are you ready to get started? Let's go!

Chapter 1
Introducing the Mat!

Cricket is watching with interest as this strange new mat floats down to the ground

So let's get cracking.

There are some things you're going to need to ensure success with these lessons, so I'll introduce them to you now.

What do you need?

Your Mat

You will only use this mat for relax and settle work. After every training session, put it away. (I'll explain why in a minute.) So you don't want to use your dog's bed. You also won't have much success with a towel or blanket - they'll get screwed up and in a mess in no time. Something flat, small, and reasonably stiff will fit the bill.

An ideal mat is a soft doormat with nonslip backing (inexpensive), or you can use a carpet sample (often free) from a carpet shop. These are usually neatly bound all around the edge.

As far as size goes, you want a mat that's big enough for the dog to sit on but not much bigger. Remember it's not a bed, so she doesn't have to fit completely on the mat. That's probably a relief to hear if you have a Deerhound or a Pyrenean Mountain Dog! The smaller the mat is, the easier it'll be to carry around with you when you are out.

Treats

The treats need to be very tasty - your dog has got to really want them! You don't want her chewing and chomping on a biscuit for so long that she forgets what she earned it for! The treat needs to slip down quickly and make your dog think, "Wow! How can I get some more of that?" Your dog needs to know what you like and what does not cut it with you. So every time she does something you like, you can mark it by saying, "YES!" and giving her a treat.

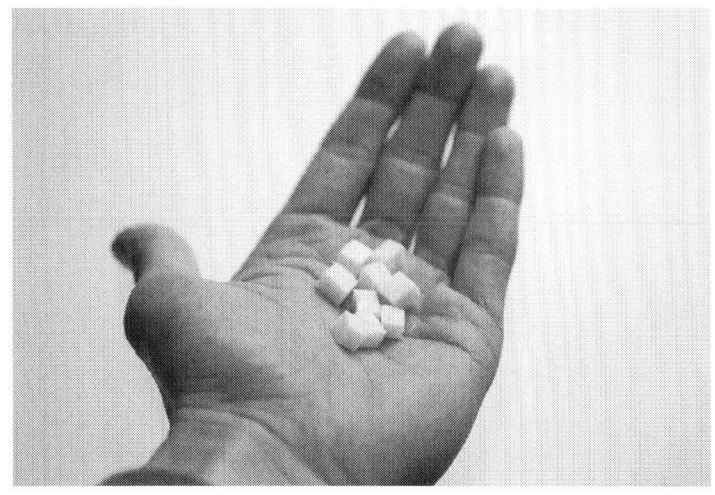

Small, tasty, treats!

Good treats

- Cheese
- Sausage
- Ham
- Chicken
- Frankfurter
- Salami
- Homemade sardine, tuna, or ham cookies
- Freeze-dried 100% meat treats
- Dehydrated liver, heart, lung, etc

…real food in other words. Ideally, they slip down quickly so your dog wants more. Cut them up small - just pea-size will do nicely.

OK treats

- High-quality grain-free commercial treats

Fairly rubbish treats

- Your dog's usual kibble (She gets it anyway. Why should she have to work for it?)
- Cat biscuits
- Dog biscuits
- Stuff of unrecognisable composition sold as pet treats
- Anything you wouldn't put in your own mouth

Do you work more enthusiastically for £60 an hour or for 50p an hour? Quite so. Your dog is the same. Be sure the treats you're offering are worth working for!

Troubleshooting

Why do I have to keep giving my dog treats? Shouldn't she do what she's told anyway?

I only give my dogs a treat when they've done something I like. I aim to get through a lot of treats every day! Treats are not a moral issue. They are a means to an end. The end is your dog calmly relaxing on her mat. If employing a few bits of cheese means that my outings are enjoyable and my visitors unmolested then that's a good deal to me.

But isn't all this extra food bad for him?

You're using high-quality food for treats. It's not like giving chocolate to a child. You have to feed your dog anyway, so you may as well get some mileage from it. If your dog is overweight, simply remove an equivalent amount of food from his dinner.

Your sessions will be really short - a minute or two at the most - so you'll only need about 20-30 little treats. Later on in your training, you could use your dog's dinner, fed morsel by morsel.

Chapter 2
Starting with the Mat

The treat goes right on the mat, between your dog's paws

Read this chapter through to the end before getting started with your dog - you want to make sure it's fresh in your mind. In fact, leave this page open so you can quickly refer to it if you lose the thread.

Have several treats ready in your hand for quick-fire delivery.

Lesson 1
Front paws on the Mat

1. Call your dog over and give her a treat to show her that something interesting is going on.

2. Now, with a flourish, produce your lovely new mat from behind your back and float it to the floor in front of her nose.

3. When she looks at the mat, immediately place a treat on it. This first treat is a reward for your dog interacting with the mat simply by looking at it.

4. As she steps onto the mat to get that treat - bang! - place a treat between her paws on the mat. While she's eating that treat, if she still has her paws on the mat, she gets another, and another. The treats should flow very fast. A good rate of delivery is one every two seconds. Your dog is being rewarded simply for having her front paws on the mat. *Note: Each treat goes on the mat between her paws. All you want to focus on in this lesson is Front Paws on the Mat. Everything else your dog learns will follow from this step.*

5. After giving her three or four treats, pause for two seconds (just two seconds - no more!) to see what she does. Your dog will probably do one of these three things:

    a. She'll stay exactly where she is. Excellent! Reward her with three more quick treats.

    b. She wanders off. *Wait.* Stand by the mat to give her time to realise that you still have good treats to be eaten. If she seems to have lost the plot, you can move round the mat to make sure it's between her and you - if necessary make a kissy noise to get her attention back. She'll most likely wander back and by accident or design she'll put her front feet on the mat. Hooray! You're back in business. Give her three or four treats between the paws, just as before.

c. She looks at you in puzzlement, wondering why you've stopped dishing out the treats. She may jump up on you: stand still and ignore her entirely. She may bark at you: look away and ignore her entirely. She may paddle her feet: wait. And she may sit: Jackpot! - give her three or four very quick treats on the mat between her paws!

Sooner or later, in this first quick session, your dog will sit. If that doesn't happen, simply repeat Steps 3 and 4 until she does sit. Just front paws on the mat no longer pays. You've moved the goalposts: *she now needs to sit with front paws on the mat.*

This is your new criterion. Sitting on the mat is what now pays, and nowhere have you told your dog to do anything!

To end your minute-long session, toss a treat away from the mat, and then pick up the mat when the dog is off it.

She's worked hard! So have a game with her with a toy.

You need to repeat this very short session several times, over several days, until when you get your mat out you have difficulty getting it to the floor because your dog is trying to leap onto it! Without telling her to do anything, she's learnt that the mat is a great place to be. Standing on it is good, and sitting on it is even more productive.

One thing I hope you've noticed during this first stage is how your dog stops dancing around, gazes at you questioningly, and *thinks*. You can see the wheels turning while she tries to solve this new puzzle you've set her. She slows down and makes thoughtful responses.

You may find that she is very tired after a couple of minutes of playing this new game. She's been thinking hard, and thinking is hard work. Encourage her to rest and let her brain file away what she's just learnt.

Troubleshooting

My dog has no interest in the mat!

At your next session, get her playing with you first. If it doesn't get her over-excited, you could run round the room with her or play with a toy. You can ramp up the energy and excitement. This should make her interested in what you're doing with this mat-thing.

Another method to try is to throw a treat on the floor for her to grab, then another the opposite way. Then slap your mat down right in her path. Be very quick to put the treat on it where she's looking. Work fast!

My dog is too distracted to look at the mat.

Choose a time when he's more likely to pay attention to you and your good food. Wait till the children are occupied quietly in another room. Maybe before his dinner, when the household is quiet, when he's not too tired, and when he's hungry. Make sure you have treats that he finds very exciting.

When I put the mat on the floor, my dog steps on it, then gets off again, and looks worried.

First, it's great that she steps on it! It's possible you aren't being quick enough with your treat. While you're standing and holding the mat, get your brain in gear, ensure you have a treat in your other hand and that your dog is paying attention to what's about to happen. Then whack down your mat and shoot your treat down between her paws as soon as she even looks at the mat. Then another and another. Do not miss her first response! We are teaching our dog to think and experiment. Your dog thought she should put her feet on the mat, but you were too slow to reward her so she thought she had made a mistake. So she backed off, and looked worried wondering what she should do.

If it helps, rehearse the steps by yourself beforehand when she isn't in the room.

She sits or stands beside the mat, but she won't get on it.

Be sure to place the treat - quickly - on the mat as soon as she looks at it. If the mat is small and the dog large, put the treat on the far side of the mat so there's a good chance she'll step on it, so you can reward Front Paws on the Mat.

He actually treats the mat as a force field and avoids stepping on it!

It's possible the mat may have some unpleasant scent on it that is putting him off. Try using other flat things and textures to see what he's happy to step on. If he likes lying on his bed or a sunny spot in the room, trying putting the mat there just to help him get started.

She stands on the mat alright, but when she sits, she moves backwards so her paws move off the mat.

Good girl! She's trying hard to do what you want! Encourage her to move a little further forward on the mat by placing the treats in front of her paws instead of between them, then when she sits she should still keep her feet on the mat. If she always paddles backwards when she sits, you could do a separate session or two practicing sits with her back to a wall. This will keep her from moving backwards, which is a habit she has formed at some point, and she'll learn to sit straight away,

My floor is all carpeted. How can she tell when she's on the mat?

Good question! Dogs' paws are very sensitive, but if the mat you've chosen feels exactly the same as your carpet in texture, simply flip the mat over. Working with the mat the wrong way up, she'll get the rough side (if carpet sample) or rubber backing (if a mat), and will clearly feel the difference in surface.

He sits on the mat, but hops up again.

When you put the treat between their paws for sitting, a few dogs will hop up again and stand to eat the treat. In this case, as soon as he sits feed his treat to his mouth (then another, then another) rather than putting them on the mat. If he hops up, stop the treat flow. He'll soon get the message that treats come only when he's sitting.

My dog is looking quite anxious about all this.

Give her a break and try again later. Make sure your sessions are short. I would suggest two minutes max. Ensure that you have good treats that she really wants (skip the biscuits - use proper food), and be very generous with your speed. One treat every two seconds is a good rate.

I thought we were doing ok then she stood and barked at me!

You probably have a quick dog who thinks you aren't going fast enough! Or maybe she's a bit confused about what she's meant to do and she's barking out of frustration. Toss a treat off the mat for her and just start again from the beginning. Be quick with giving her a treat, and get it to her before she draws breath to bark. You can quickly separate the bark from the "being on the mat," then you can carry on.

I have to wave a treat in front of him to get him to come to the mat.

This is called luring, and while luring has its place in dog training, its place is not here! We're not trying to coax him onto the mat. If you need food to get your dog to come to you, two things can go wrong.

First, you are giving him a choice. Giving him a choice is good only as long as you don't lose out! You are asking him, "Do you want to stay where you are, or do you want this treat?"

What do you do if he decides to stay where he is?

Second, if you have to show him the colour of your money before you ask for anything, he'll soon learn that if you don't have food you are powerless and not worth bothering with.

As if those two things aren't bad enough, there's also the fact that he won't be choosing to go on the mat - he'll just be following his nose for the treat in front of it and he'll have no idea where he's going at all! This is just like when we drive following another car. We're so concerned with keeping the car in our sights that we have little idea where we actually are and are none the wiser about our route when we arrive at our destination. It's essential that your dog chooses to go on the mat, by himself. Choice is very important in all of these lessons!

In this Chapter we have established that:

- The mat is a touchpad. When your dog's paws are on it, treats magically appear between them
- Doing something new brings rewards. She doesn't have to wait to be told to do something
- Doing something different brings more rewards. We're building an enquiring mind here
- Working very quickly is essential to keep the flow
- "I can think for myself!" she says as she hops onto the mat and claims her reward!

Chapter 3
Mat Magic!

Bailey (15 weeks) relaxes at Puppy Class

So now, when you bring out the mat and swoosh it to the floor, your dog leaps straight on it. Let's move on to some more mat magic!

Your dog clearly understands that sitting on the mat results in good things. The next stage is to get her to lie down on the mat.

In the same way that we haven't yet told the dog to do anything at all - we've just waited for her to make good choices that she finds pay - we won't be telling her to sit or lie down either. You probably got her sitting on the mat in the last few sessions. If not, just continue the very short mat sessions till she gets it. When she eventually lowers herself into a sit - throw a party! Cheer, dance, throw treats, and then end the session.

We've moved the goalposts once - so that the dog is now being paid for sitting - and now we're going to move them again.

Lesson 2
Down on the Mat

After a few speedy sits and treats from Lesson 1, you can now expect your dog to lie down.

1. Simply break your rhythm and pause in the same way as you did to achieve a Sit.

    a. Your dog may wiggle her bottom or paddle her feet to check she's sitting already: wait. She may try a different place on the mat: ignore what you don't want and keep waiting. If she seems anxious, go back to rewarding her for sitting, then try again a little later. You don't need to maintain a stony silence! Some encouraging noises are good so she doesn't get worried and give up, but at all costs resist the temptation to tell her what to do!

    b. She may bark or poke you to say, "Hey, I'm sitting!" Ignore these actions and wait. Wait for a good decision from her.

    c. She may move a front paw forward while she considers changing position, YES! treat, treat, treat between the paws! You don't need to wait for a full Down – just a slight move in the right direction is rewardable. She will probably complete the down action to get at the treats. Stop the treat flow as soon as she sits up again.

2. Repeat this stage several times over the next few days to establish that the default position on the mat now is to lie down.

Keep your sessions very short. Kettle time is always a good opportunity for a quick training session. While you wait for the kettle to boil, grab a small handful of tasty treats, toss the mat on the floor and you're off!

How do I get my dog to lie down?

By this stage, your dog will be flying to her mat and landing on it in a down position. Just sometimes, though, especially with very small dogs, they don't get that they need to move on from a sit to a down position - or they lie the front half down and the tail end pops up into the air! If your dog is not lying down there are a few things we can do to teach her. The first one you can do on the mat, the others anywhere.

Teaching her Down on the mat

1. When you place the food between her paws, keep your hand over it so she has to get her head down and burrow in under your hand to reach the treat. Quite soon she'll need to move a front paw forward to help her bend - Yes! Treat! Next time you can wait till the paw moves a little further forward and her elbow touches the mat - Yes! Treat!

2. Repeat this till you have both elbows on the mat, then treat, treat, treat, break, and have a game.

You don't have to wait for a complete Down to reward and encourage her - just a tiny move in the direction of a Down will do.

Capture a Down

1. Choose a time when you can relax and your puppy is playing with her toys.

2. Keep an eye on her and when she eventually lies down, say "Yes!" and ask her to come over for a treat. She won't know why she's being rewarded yet, but that doesn't matter. After a while she'll lie down again - "Yes!" - she gets up and comes over to you for another treat. Let her wander off again. To begin with these events may be ten minutes apart.

3. Watch carefully, as at some stage your puppy will twig what's happening and tentatively slide a paw forward and start to lower herself to the floor: "Yes!!" Party! She's got it!

4. Now you can start adding the word "Down." Only say it once, just as she's about to lie down. In one short session you have a puppy who will lie down when you ask.

Lie down in a tunnel

The tunnel can be furniture - a chair cross-bar just the right height for your dog to lie under may work well - or your legs.

1. Sit on the floor with your legs stretched out in front of you.
2. Raise your knees and make a big tunnel.
3. With your dog on your left, put your right hand loaded with a treat under your knees and draw her through, giving her the treat as she emerges the other side.
4. After running her through the tunnel a couple of times she will learn it's a game and not a trap. Now repeat it, but lower your knees slightly so she has to crawl through.
5. As soon as her bum goes to the floor you can release your treat. Once this is happening every time you can label this action of hers as "Down".

Luring

1. Put the treat to her nose so that her nose is touching your hand.
2. Lower your hand slowly, keeping the nose attached. Move it slightly down and into the dog so that it takes her nose down between her paws.
3. Give her a treat.

4. Next one, wait for the front legs to bend a little so the elbows come down.

5. Give her a treat. And so on.

6. Once the elbows are fully on the floor, her bottom will collapse down.

Occasionally a dog will remain in a play-bow and resolutely refuse to lower her rear end. Worry not! Just give this a suitable name like "Take a bow" just as she's doing it, and you now have a cute trick. Try one of the other methods to achieve your Down.

Luring can work, but you must stop offering food in the hand that was holding it as soon as she's got the idea. You still reward your dog with a treat for doing what you want, but after she's done it, not before.

Troubleshooting

My dog will lie down on the mat, but she bounces straight back up again!

That sounds as if she's got the idea to lie down but she doesn't realise she needs to stay down. You're obviously doing very well so far. Have a few treats ready in your hand. Don't use a pot or bag as you want to be able to react as soon as she even starts to move into a down position. Once she lies down, you can start shovelling the treats into her mouth, one, two, three … As long as she's down you keep posting the treats in. As soon as she lifts up the treats stop again.

My dog is off and on the mat the whole time.

If your dog is on the mat, off the mat, back on the mat to get a treat, off again, back on for a treat, etc, you're building a chain of actions that you don't want! If he leaves the mat then comes back - it's not bad or wrong, it's just not going to earn a treat. So when he steps back on, tell him how good he is, wait for a second or so, then reward him. He'll soon learn stepping off the mat delays the rewards and opt to stay put.

I've got her to lie down by luring her. How do I stop having to move her down with the treat?

Nice work! When you use a lure to get your dog to do something, it's essential that you stop luring as soon as possible. See the last Troubleshooting Question and Answer in Chapter 2: Starting with the Mat, which explains it fully. Instead, wait and let your dog work it out.

I put the mat on the floor and my dog says, "So?"

If your dog is not interested in the mat, it means you haven't built up a strong enough association that Mat = Good Things. Go back to the beginning - you can run through this very quickly - and be sure that first your dog is hungry and not too tired, second the environment is quiet, calm, and not distracting, and - most important! - you're using small treats that he thinks are *divine*.

We've taught the dog to love getting on to her mat. The next step is to teach how to get *off* the mat. She can't just get up and mosey off when she feels like it. Once she's on the mat, she has to stay there till you release her.

Lesson 3
Learning when to get off the mat

You have just rewarded your dog quickly several times in a row for lying down on her mat.

1. Keeping the same rhythm, and without moving away from the mat, hold your hand out with a treat at dog-nose level a yard or so from the mat and say, "Break." Your dog will bounce off the mat to sniff your hand and eat the treat. Now stand up and *wait*. What's going to happen next?

a. If you've kept the rhythm going there's a high chance that your dog will bounce straight back on to her mat. Yes! Treat! Wait for her to lie down - more treats!

b. She bounces off the mat for her treat in your hand, then she stops, unsure what to do next. *Wait.* Let her work it out. Chances are she'll suddenly remember where she was getting all those rewards and step back onto her mat. If she seems anxious, make encouraging noises till she at least looks at the mat - Yes! Treat on the mat! We're off again.

c. She wanders off to see if there are more treats on the ground. If you have any idea this may happen, practice with a long lead on the dog and your foot on the end of it. This will limit her wanderings to the area near the mat. *Wait* and change your position if necessary so you are the opposite side of the mat from her. At some stage she is going to wander back towards you and accidentally put her paws on the mat - Yes! Treat! Now we're back in business.

2. Practice breaks now and then, but most of the treats your dog gets should still be between the paws on the mat. At least six rewards for lying down on the mat before you do another break. We want the association with the mat to be lying down and keeping still, not bouncing on and off!

From now on, whenever you want your dog off the mat - and certainly at the end of the short session - you can "break" her. Don't forget to have a quick game with her - she's worked hard for you.

As you continue with these sessions you'll find that your dog is happy to wait till she hears her release word. All she has to do is stay there and wait for the rewards to trickle in. She's quite clear in what she needs to do.

I was working with my dog Lacy while making coffee one day. She was lying nicely on her mat and getting rewarded from time to time. Suddenly there was a hullabaloo from the garden - the hens were squawking, and the other dogs flew out to see what was going on. We had a visiting dog, and I thought he may have been upsetting the hens, so I raced out too. It was just a couple of hens having an argument - the visiting dog was innocent. Everyone calmed down. When I strolled back in to get my coffee, there was Lacy, lying still on her mat amidst all the kerfuffle and excitement! Yes, I'd entirely forgotten her in the moment. But what a good girl!

That's the power of teaching your dog to stay on the mat until told otherwise. She was quite clear that what she was doing was keeping that mat still under her.

Troubleshooting

Do I have to use the word "break"?

You can use absolutely any word you like! I'd avoid "okay" because we say that a million times a day and this can lead to confusion. You want a word which only means "you're released from the thing I asked you to do." Make it crystal clear. When I say, "Break," my dogs don't run away from the mat, they run over to me to see what's next.

Just when it seems to be going well, she wanders off the mat.

I'd guess that you've slowed down a bit with the treats, so perhaps she thinks you've finished. In the first place, keep up a steady flow of treats when she's doing what you want. Practice your break so she's quite clear when she can move off. Keep your sessions very short!

My dog keeps licking her lips. Does this mean she likes the treats a lot? She's quite shy at the best of times.

Lip-licking, along with yawning when not tired, avoiding eye contact, looking away - among other gestures - is what's known as a calming signal. These are easily read by other, socially-skilled, dogs, but not so well read by us dog owners! It's a sign of slight anxiety. She's worried she's doing the wrong thing.

Whenever a dog is anxious, the best thing is to back off or ease up a little. Bring some more joy and lightness to your sessions. Keep them incredibly short (maybe 6 treats), and be sure to play with your dog as a big reward after!

She takes ages to come back on the mat and goes off sniffing instead.

She seems distracted. The treats should be so delicious that she can't wait to get back on the mat to get another. Make sure the floor is clear of toys and crumbs or other small distractions. Be sure the environment is not distracting - the children playing noisily outside for instance - and put her on a six-foot lead which you can put your foot on so she can't go wandering off.

All these treats! Do I have to give them forever?

That's such a good question! Treats - in fact anything the dog finds pleasurable - are invaluable for teaching the dog something new. Look at it this way: you've got to feed your dog anyway, so why not get some mileage from the food? If you put all the food in a bowl, put it down and walk away, you are missing a huge learning opportunity for your dog! As you become skilled as a trainer, you'll know when to speed up and when to slow down the number of treats. You'll also learn to vary the type of rewards you use. We'll look at this in more detail later on. For now, just keep dishing out the rewards whenever your dog does something you like. You'll be able to cut the treats right down later - but not yet. Don't push the scaffolding away too soon!

In this Chapter we have established that:

- The mat represents a very special place in your dog's eyes
- It pleases you enormously when she puts her paws on it
- She looks forward to you getting the mat out as it's a guaranteed way to get rewards
- Your dog needs to anchor the mat to the floor so the rewards can keep coming
- Helping your dog will actually slow down her rate of learning
- "I can make good decisions!"

Chapter 4
What do I do with this mat now?

Lacy relaxes on her mat while I enjoy coffee and a good book

Let's look now at what you can do next. You have taught your dog a game with the mat which she looks forward to and engages in with enthusiasm. You have built this up in stages with clarity. Now we can take it on the road!

Coffee with a friend, or Sunday lunch at the pub

Now you've got this working smoothly at home, start taking it out of the house to new places. Keep your first trip fairly short. Start by going to a place you already know.

Let's say you're meeting a friend at a café. There are plenty of good cafés that will allow dogs - many welcome them. The same goes for pubs. In fact you'll find internet resources that list dog-friendly eateries. I have a printout of dog-friendly venues for my locality that I keep in the car. If I want to stop somewhere for a meal or a break, I can go straight to a suitable café or hostelry, without having to go in first and ask if I may bring the dog in.

Even those who don't want dogs inside are usually happy for you to sit at an outside table with your dog.

Treat your dog just as you would a toddler, and set out on your journey well-equipped. Bring her mat, really good treats, chews, a filled food toy, a favourite teddy bear … Be sure you have plenty of things to distract her with. It will really help if your friend is willing to allow you to focus on your dog whenever necessary.

1. Give her a run or an exciting game beforehand so she's ready to settle down.
2. Choose a spot to place the mat where your dog won't get trodden on. Avoid high traffic areas, such as near the main door, the toilets, and the kitchens. These places are too busy.
3. Then simply reward your dog with good things as soon as she puts herself on the mat. You'll have her on a lead, of course, but make sure it's loose enough for her to be able to find a comfortable position, while you have the handle firmly in your hand.

Never tie your dog to a table or chair - that's far too risky. Just have the lead on your wrist then you'll be aware straight away if she's getting agitated for any reason. Maybe when your dog is as experienced as Lacy is, you can attach the lead to a suitable fixed point - like a very heavy chair.

On this first occasion you may spend more time making sure your dog is content than chatting to your friend. But this is insurance! Next time will be much easier. Once your first trip has been successful, you can try different places. Soon your dog will be able to go anywhere with you - settling down and amusing herself without annoying you or anybody else. This is one good reason for having a small, easily transportable mat. Once your Mat Magic is well-established, anything will do for a mat.

My son and I were out walking and found a pub showing a cricket match on tv, so in we went to have a quick lunch. Sky the Whippet was with us. She was tired, but the floors were hard, and - as you may know - thin-skinned whippets love their comfort! She really wanted to lie down, but did not want to rest on floorboards. You could as well have asked her to lie down on a bed of nails. It was a hot summer's day, so we had no jumpers or coats we could put down for her. We were miles from the car and this was an unplanned stop so we had not brought Sky's mat. I took one of the flimsy paper serviettes provided with our meal, opened it out and put it on the floor. With relief, Sky lay straight down on it and rested.

A peaceful evening in the living room

Probably the first and easiest way most people will use their mat is to encourage their dog to settle in the living room of an evening. If your dog has been accustomed to jumping around and pestering you whenever you take to your armchair, you will love this! If your dog already has a bed in the living room, then you can transfer to that after you've established the new setup, but begin with the mat.

1. Be sure your dog has had a good game in the garden or that she's had a walk. She needs something to puff her out before you ask her to settle down.

2. Sit in your chair, put the mat on the floor beside you, and place the reward between her paws as usual. This time you can use your dog's dinner. Feed one morsel at a time. You can also use treats, but use fairly boring ones, like her kibble.

3. As you both settle for the evening, you'll find your rate of reward naturally slowing down.

4. Don't forget to "break" your dog when you've had enough. She can leave her mat if she wants to, or she can stay zizzing. "Break" just means you have released her from the session and she can do what she wants.

To begin with, do this just for a few minutes. After a few sessions, over a few days, you can start working a bit longer. You can have chews or food toys to keep her occupied then.

Incidentally, to add a vocal cue for the mat, just say "Mat," "Bed," "Chill," "Settle" - whatever you want - quietly, exactly as your dog is stepping onto the mat. You're describing her action. That's how dogs make the connection between the word and the deed. They don't have verbal language like we do, but they can associate a sound with an action (think doorbell). After doing this for a while, you can say your cue just as she's thinking about going on the mat.

One golden advantage of my dogs being happy to go on their mats is this: if my four dogs are pacing or playing in the living room when I want some peace and quiet, I just say, "Bed!" and they all go straight to the nearest bed and lie down. There is such a strong history of reward from parking themselves on something – be it a mat, a stool, or a garden chair – that they don't see it as a punishment.

Dogs need a huge amount of sleep, so as long as they've had entertainment and activity in the day there's no need for them to keep going all evening. Indeed, keeping going is a bad idea, because they will get ragged, frustrated, and difficult. Value sleep!

Visiting the vet

Your dog will have to visit the vet from time to time. She's already experienced a trip to the vet, and she'll already have an opinion about it.

If you've developed a good relationship with your vet and staff, your dog may eagerly bounce into the waiting room - seeing it as a purely social visit. Some dogs though, may have had to undergo painful procedures or have had poor experiences with other dogs in the waiting room while awaiting their turn. If this is the case with your dog, you may need to rebuild her confidence.

The smell of the vet's clinic is very strong and particular to that place. Just walking to the door, your dog will know where she is. When you think of ice cream, maybe it triggers your earliest memories - connecting it to the seaside or a childhood visit to Granny's. Tastes and smells can evoke very strong feelings. The dog's taste and smell mechanisms are thousands of times more powerful than ours! So we want to make sure that strong smell of the vet's is associated with not only good experiences but also a state of calm and relaxation. So whether your dog is a social butterfly or is anxious - wide-eyed and panting - at the vet's, the foundation you've built with your mat will greatly contribute to this calm and relaxed state.

By the way, my dogs are encouraged to acknowledge people when they're in the vet's waiting room, but I don't let them interact with any other animals that may be there. Why are those animals there? Well, they could be sick, they could be contagious, they could be flea-ridden, they could be in pain. Not a good basis for meeting another dog. Keeping your dog to yourself is a very important piece of etiquette for vet visits.

Take your mat with you, along with a few other things to amuse your dog if you anticipate a long wait. Put the mat on the floor beside you. On goes your dog, and assuming the vet visit will not entail anaesthetic (so eating beforehand is ok), on go your treats. Quite soon you have a contented happy dog who is not anxiously scanning the room to see who may be coming in next.

Other clients will more than likely admire what you are doing and try to get their dog to calm a little too. Sadly, they won't have your Magic Mat Recipe, so they'll probably employ a lot of lead-yanking, nagging, and complaining, which won't get them very far.

When it's time to go in to see the vet, you can "break" your dog off the mat and take it with you into the examination room. While you are talking to the vet your dog can be lying on her mat at your feet - rather than lurching and pulling on the lead, trying to stick her nose in the sharps bin and so on. You will be maintaining the calm and relaxed state the mat induced out in the waiting room. When it's time, you can break your dog off the mat, lift her onto the table and carry on treating her for staying still while she is examined and assessed by the vet.

Not only will you be bursting with pride that your dog is so well behaved in a potentially stressful situation, but others will notice too.

Amanda and Harley, her labradoodle pup and one of my Puppy Class students - proudly told me about her puppy's vet visit. She found the waiting room very busy, with dogs whining. Harley lay quietly on his mat chewing a chewtoy. No-one could believe that he was only five months old and so calm and well-behaved.

"That mat is going everywhere with us from now on!" Amanda said.

Harley (20 weeks) in the vet's waiting room, showing how it's done

Seeing is believing. You have to try things to find out just how well they work. Amanda believes in her mat!

By the way - if you don't have any vet visits scheduled, you can always drop in at a time when they're not too busy, greet the receptionist, and do a little mat practice in the waiting room. Vet staff are usually very pleased at anything owners do to keep their pet calm on a visit. It's no fun for them to wrestle with a distressed dog when they're trying to help. So they will be happy for you to do this - if a little bemused!

Family picnic

You've probably been somewhere new and exciting - the beach, a forest, open fields - and the children and your family dog have played themselves to a standstill.

Time for the picnic.

While you spread out the food on the cloth or table, put out the cushions or chairs, and settle down to eat, you don't want to have to be on edge the whole time wondering where on earth your dog has gone. For those of you with foodaholic dogs, you don't want their eyes and nose following every morsel you put in your mouth.

Put the mat on the ground near you, but just far enough away that she won't be tempted to snaffle your sandwiches. Have her on a loose lead as well, but the mat will telling her to stay put. Occasional treats may help, but a food-filled toy will certainly focus her mind on staying where she is until she dozes off.

Once the children have refuelled, you can break her off the mat so you can all carry on the games. Meanwhile she's had a good rest - hopefully a sleep too, and is ready for more play without getting ragged and over-excited.

In this Chapter we have learnt that:

- The mat can go with you anywhere
- It is a safe haven
- It becomes self-rewarding - you can slow the treats right down
- You can all relax
- "I can enjoy being out with the family without bouncing all the time!"

Chapter 5
Taking it on the road

Coco waits on his mat while I answer the doorbell

Let's explore now all the ways your mat can help you in your daily life with your family dog. Once you've established the mat as a safe place for her to park herself - for as long as you want her parked - the way is opened for you to use it in many different interactions with your dog. It becomes a normal part of the dog's response. Instead of leaping and bounding around aimlessly, she'll know that putting herself on her mat is a wise choice and may well earn her rewards.

How about a situation which is a big problem for many dog-owners? A ring at the doorbell.

The doorbell!

The doorbell can send many dogs into a state of extreme excitement which makes them very hard to control. You may grab your dog by the collar to try to answer the door with your arm being yanked up and down by a demented dog. You may just open the door a crack because your dog is fearful of strangers and may decide to "have a go." Perhaps you just resort to shutting her in another room.

How about this instead?

1. Teach your dog that when the doorbell rings, she runs to her mat and will be rewarded mightily for that. This may take you a week or two. If you focus on it for a week you may be amazed how good she gets! You do it when there aren't any real visitors, just you and her, and perhaps a useful third person to stay outside and ring the bell periodically. You are simply teaching her that the sound of the doorbell is the signal for her to race to her mat, lie down, and stay there for the flow of rewards.

2. Once you've got this stage down, you may set things up so you can stay by your dog, feeding her treats, while someone else answers the door. Keep it all very brief and good fun.

3. Now when the doorbell rings, your dog will go to her mat and wait patiently for the treats to start appearing. If you're a good shot and the mat is well positioned in sight of the door, you can buzz treats to her while you speak to your caller. This will gradually become her default behaviour on hearing the bell.

If this is a major and well-established problem at your home, there are a couple of gadgets that can help you with this.

For the training: A wireless doorbell (very cheap). You can place the amplifier wherever you want, stand right by the mat, and just hold the button in your hand and press it. This allows you to be right on top of the situation. As soon as the doorbell rings your dog hops on her mat and you can post the treats into your dog without delay.

For the real thing: A Manners Minder or Treat'n'Train (not so cheap). This is a remote controlled device that administers treats either as you press the remote button or on a set schedule of your choosing. This is especially useful if your dog is fearful and anxious about visitors. She'll be paying attention to the dispensing machine and not worrying about the person at the door. At my house, once the machine is switched on, my anxious dog Lacy stays rivetted in front of it, her nose hovering over the dispenser tray, despite the two-headed monsters at the door!

Targets

Not the sort you have to achieve at work, more the archery sort with a bull's eye. The mat is what's known technically as a "target behaviour." That is to say, the dog is targetting the mat with her front feet. As we've seen, this leads to a Down and ultimately a relaxed state.

You can transfer this targetting to any object you like: another bed in the house, your lap (for very small dogs!), a footstool, in the back of the car where your dog travels, your jumper on the floor (for when you forget your mat, like I did with Sky the Whippet), and so on.

Your dog has learnt to stay on the mat till you release her with "Break".

So how about this for calm exits from the house?

1. Strategically place your mat a couple of yards in front of the door.
2. Put the lead on your dog and walk towards the door.
3. She should see the mat and sit or lie down on it without needing to be told, but she may be excited that you're going for a walk and you may need to remind her.

4. Put your hand on the door handle and if necessary ask her to sit.

5. Open the door a crack, shut it again, say, "break," and toss a treat away behind her so she gets up to eat the treat, then comes back to her mat and sits as you put your hand on the handle again.

6. Keep going with short sessions, opening the door a little more each time until you're able to open the door fully without her shifting from her mat.

7. Open the door wide, pause for a moment, then break her to step outside with you. No mad crashing the door and yanking your arm. If the prospect of the walk is too exciting for your dog to focus, start by using an inner door - a bedroom door or some other non-exciting doorway.

And this one, for the car?

1. Your dog is in your car, restrained of course, either in a crate or with a harness and lead.

2. You open the car door. Dog sits patiently.

3. You open the crate door, reach in and attach the lead, or switch the car restraint for your walking lead. Dog continues to sit patiently.

4. Now, when the coast is clear and the road safe, you can give your release word, "Break."

5. Out hops your dog.

6. If you really want to make this perfect and dazzle everyone watching, you can have her mat ready on the ground so she immediately parks herself on that mat and sits waiting - still patiently - for you to shut the door, lock the car, and start on your walk. You'll be able to skip the second mat once this is a habit.

Preparing dinner

This is one use of the Magic Mat that I absolutely love. There are few things more annoying than trying to cook dinner while your dog gets under your feet to trip you up (very dangerous too with hot pans involved), or finding your elbow continually nudged by a searching nose, or worst of all, turning to get a knife to cut the meat, then turning back to find the meat gone. All this can be solved with your mat!

1. Choose a convenient place for the mat. I suggest somewhere out of your way but close enough that your dog can still see you.

2. Load a food toy with goodies (possibly your dog's dinner), and prepare your meal without help from your four-footed, begging friend.

3. Always remember to break your dog when she's allowed off her mat. If she comes off without permission, I would just stand still, say "Where are you meant to be?" and wait for her to return. Once she puts herself back on the mat you can tell her how clever she is and carry on as before. Like us, dogs take pride in working out puzzles and doing something they know to be right.

Mat substitutes

One of the great benefits of teaching your dog to love her mat is that you can transfer what she does on the mat to any other object you name a "mat".

You can use a doormat, a low wall, a barrel, a box, a mounting-block, a boulder, a tree stump, a chair, a picnic table, a step, a raised bed, an armchair, or - as in the case of Sky the Whippet - a paper square! Really, you can use anything that has a defined edge or border.

After a 5-mile walk with my gang we stopped at a café. No, I was not going to carry four mats in my backpack! I knew I'd find something suitable to ground them for a few minutes. Sure enough, there was an umbrella over the table outside the café. It had a large weighted base a few inches high - just big enough to accommodate four tired dogs!

You can usually find something to make into an honorary mat, wherever you go.

Reports from the Front Line

Here are some comments from students in my puppy classes, where matwork with all its applications is an important component:

> "Here is Samson being as good as gold in the pub this afternoon after Puppy Class - mat and food toy used to full effect!"
>
> Anna and Samson the Rhodesian Ridgback puppy

And Ellen, who travels a lot with her work - and takes her Border Collie puppy with her - told me:

> "The mat has helped greatly with making puppy trips easier and laying the foundations of good communication. Selkie's particularly great on her mat on buses, trains and in pubs!"

Finally, Wendy and Mike were delighted when their very active Vizsla pup learnt how to settle down on her mat:

"We've just come back from a couple of days on our narrowboat and Roux was so good! We went to a couple of pubs en route and used the mat and treats and she was as good as gold: she even went to sleep on it in a very noisy pub, ignoring yappy dogs and loud noises!"

I've given you a complete road map with detailed directions and GPS coordinates! Start from the beginning and follow the plan. Whenever something is not quite right, go back a step or two to where it was right, and move forward again.

In this Chapter we have established that:

- The mat can be used to get a number of calm responses - use your imagination!
- Your dog knows she's doing the right thing so there's no confusion
- Your dog can stay in any place you choose until you release her with "break!"
- It makes life much simpler and your dog's responses more consistent
- "I can wait patiently - I'm learning impulse control!"

Chapter 6
Surprise benefits of Mat Magic!

8-week-old Finley spark out on his mat in the living room

Your dog will now put herself on her mat, lie down, and wait. This is gradually going to turn into an action that sees your dog get on mat, lie down, R-E-L-A-X. You can teach your dog to totally relax at the flip of a switch.

Have you ever envied those people who, when finding they have to wait five or ten minutes for something, can just switch off and nap for a few minutes? They wake up refreshed and relaxed, ready to face whatever the world throws at them.

We were once travelling on a long car journey with a very successful businessman. He suddenly pulled over to a quiet spot at the side of the road and said, "I'm going to sleep for five minutes." He let his head loll and fell instantly asleep! Five minutes later, he opened his eyes, switched on the engine, and we continued our journey with a refreshed and renewed driver.

This is a skill your dog now has! And it's a skill I love to develop in my dogs.

Dogs need to sleep a massive number of hours a day. It's been established, by scientists studying stress in dogs, that the optimum number of hours of sleep for an adult dog is seventeen. Anything less and they start to get ragged. Puppies obviously need more sleep. Are you reeling from that revelation? If your dog is getting much less than seventeen hours you need to make some changes.

One of the huge advantages of the Magic Mat is that every time your dog gets on it she is relaxing and de-stressing. Even if she only goes on it for five minutes - like my businessman friend - she's getting the benefit of complete relaxation.

While I'm at my desk, my dogs are expected to find a bed or mat to concentrate on sleeping. Their sleep may be light or deep, but the state of relaxation induced by their mat ensures that they are truly resting. They are free of anxiety and totally content. When I'm out, I also expect them to be resting on their beds. I know they do because I've left my phone recording them. I get a rivettingly boring playback of a couple of hours of silence, interrupted by the occasional stretch, yawn, or creak of a bed.

Dogs can suffer a lot of stress in our human world. Granted, they get the great benefit of shelter, healthcare, and regular food, so it's a good trade-off for them - and it's why they hooked up with us in the first place. But the stress of our high-speed schedules can take a toll. If your dog is already struggling with anxiety or reacting poorly to new situations, people, or other dogs, then the seventeen hours of restorative sleep is even more important. So if your dog spends every minute of every day actively playing with the children, pacing about while you work, going for walks, jumping about in the living room, trying to steal food from the kitchen counters, nipping at heels, ripping toys up, digging, chasing, and barking, she is NOT leading the carefree, healthy, and happy life you may imagine.

Just like with a toddler, lack of rest demands its price. A toddler will grizzle, scream, become unreasonable, throw a tantrum, be demanding, impossible to satisfy, until you put her in her cot for a couple of hours' nap. Then she'll wake and be your angelic child once more. Dogs really are the same! Without the necessary sleep their poor stressed brains become overloaded. They become frantic, totally non-amenable to reason. They ignore what you are saying. They grab, nip, bark - they are beside themselves.

The answer is to escort them straight to their crate and settle them there quickly, then leave the room to allow them to sleep.

Ideally, you should build the sleep into their daily routine from the start!

How should our day go?

To give you an idea of how I manage my four - very, very different - dogs, this is an example of a day. There is no fixed schedule as my commitments vary throughout the week, but most of these things happen at some stage in the day.

- Rise, go out to garden, relieve themselves, and run about while I feed the hens
- Lie down in my bedroom or play with teddy bears while I dress
- Go outside again while I make coffee and feed the cat
- Each day a different dog comes for a solo roadwalk with me
- Lie down on their beds or quietly chew toys while I work
- Half an hour of very active games or training
- Rest while I have lunch
- Potter about with me while I do the washing, cleaning, and other chores
- Sleep while I go out to appointments - either in their crates in the van, or at home
- Highly active long dog walk with chasing, jumping, retrieving, and recall games
- Sleep till their supper time
- Potter, sleep, a few minutes training on and off, and so on

- Bedtime in their appointed sleeping places, where they stay till morning
- Training takes place a minute at a time at any time of day; garden visits every couple of hours; spontaneous active games any time

A carefully-considered sleep routine also means that my new puppies sleep through the night from the day they arrive at 7-8 weeks. That's something I'll go into more detail with you in another place. You can see from this, that building a strong association between the mat and sleep and rest, can aid your dog in speedily getting into that valuable relaxed state.

Your dog's behaviour around the house will improve dramatically. No nagging and poking, no cruising the tables and worktops for food, no doing naughty things to get a response from you. Your life together will become so much more harmonious and responsive.

All because of your Magic Mat.

In this Chapter we have established that:

- Your mat can induce a state of deep relaxation
- This relaxation will transfer to any bed
- Stress is massively lowered
- "Zzzzzz"

Conclusion

This is just the beginning for you!

If you've been working along as you read this book, you'll already have noticed a huge improvement in your dog's calmness and responsiveness. Congratulations! Now you see how well it works, you just have to keep it going, regularly.

Don't be tempted to chuck your mat aside and think, "I've done that. What next?" Keep it near to hand and remember that it can be the solution to a lot of common household problems and hysteria.

If you have a problem you need to resolve - if your dog has started doing something that annoys or frustrates you - revisit this book and see if your mat can help you to calm and slow things down enough to re-teach something you do like.

This is just the start for you!

There are just four skills you need to turn your wild puppy into your Brilliant Family Dog. Just four. Everything else flows from these. If you have these four skills, you're done!

You have in this book one quarter of what you need to have a Brilliant Family Dog. To find the other three parts, have a look at the Resources section at the end of this book.

Resources

If you've got any specific queries, you can email me direct at beverley@brilliantfamilydog.com This will come straight to my personal inbox and I'll answer you - usually within 48 hours. Try me!

Meanwhile, for more free training, go to www.brilliantfamilydog.com and get a series of instructional emails on common day-to-day problems, like jumping up, chewing, barking, and so on.

> Your emails are absolutely wonderful! I love them. Nobody else does anything like this. Maggie and Archie

> I always enjoy reading your emails and find them really useful. Joss

> The one thing Busta wasn't so good at was greeting people, but since your email we've had everyone popping in to try and put your tips into place and it worked! Now we no longer have him jumping all over us when we come through the door. Just a very happy dog sat down waggling his tail like mad, waiting for a fuss! Charlie and Busta

> Love your Brilliant Family Dog course. I look forward to the nuggets! Jenny and Jazz

> You talk such sense! I have been using the method you talk about so I can examine my almost 10 month old Beagle's teeth and it works a treat. You have inspired me to work towards clipping her dew claws myself instead of a visit to the vet! I'll let you know how I get on. I am sure there are many of us out there in the parent doggy world needing your expert tips. Alison and her Beagle pup

Essential Skills for a Brilliant Family Dog

Book 2

Leave It!

How to teach Amazing Impulse Control
to your Brilliant Family Dog

Beverley Courtney

Introduction
Now you see it, now you don't

Gunner waits politely in front of a handful of cheese and sausage

"I only turned my back for a second," Sally wailed to me in class, "and the whole cake was gone!"

She'd left it on the kitchen worktop, out of reach of her dog Jacko - or so she thought! She came back from her phone call to see the dog in his bed, his face festooned with frosting, polishing off the last remains of the cake.

This thieving happened regularly, which showed that Sally was a bit of a slower learner than Jacko!

For some dogs it's "counter-surfing" - stealing food from the kitchen worktops. For others, it's anything they can snatch up from the floor. It could be the children's toys, stones from the drive, or ice cream from a child's hand.

Oh, and don't forget dead things they find on country walks which will make them sick on the carpet later.

There's also the safety issue of sharp things, poisonous things, and medications. It could be jumping out of the car as soon as the door is opened a crack, crashing through doors at home, barging past you on the stairs to trip you up, or leaping about like a thing possessed when you mention the word "walk". Then there's barking at the window, yipping at other dogs playing, and whining for dinner.

All stem from the same issue - lack of impulse control.

See it - gotta have it!

We have no problem teaching our children how to control their desires - so why do we struggle with dogs? Perhaps people tend to think they can't expect anything better. "It's only a dog," they tell themselves. As you probably know if you've reared children or managed staff - *what you expect is what you get!*

Dogs can learn just as well as children can. In the wild, they would need to learn self-control in order to survive in a competitive environment. Puppies learn early not to interfere with big brother's dinner, and organising a hunt can involve days of hunger, stalking, and patience. In their natural state, dogs are opportunist scavengers. A whole cake just above nose level? Obviously a prize for the dog.

There isn't a moral issue here. Until you teach her what's what, any food is fair game for your dog.

Dogs don't do things to spite their owners! Dogs do what works.

If swiping the cake off the counter tastes good, then they'll do it again and again. Why shouldn't they? But it doesn't mean that your house has to be in permanent lockdown for the next fifteen years.

- Would you like to be able to leave food out wherever you want, secure in the knowledge that your dog won't touch it?
- Would you like to have a dog who sits calmly to have the lead put on when you're getting ready for a walk?
- How about waiting at the top of the stairs to be released, rather than charging down to trip you up?
- Keeping their feet on the floor when visitors arrive?
- Or leaving those tasty and dangerous slugs and pebbles well alone?

I hear you thinking, "This must involve loads of different training techniques. I'll be forever training my dog new things when all I want is a companion dog and a quiet life!"

Nope. It's just the one thing: *Impulse Control.*

It was having to learn the techniques to make a Brilliant Family Dog with my own busy household of multiple dogs, cats, sheep, goats, hens, and children that set me on the road to helping others do the same. I learnt early on that forcing someone to do something only resulted in grudging compliance at best; whereas getting them to participate and enjoy the process turned them into eager and fast learners. This applied equally to the dogs, the goats - and the children! The sheep and the cats not so much.

My qualifications range from the understanding of learning theory to specialist work for fearful, anxious, and growly dogs. Acquiring an anxious, growly dog of my own ensured that I learnt and understood the process of assimilating the dog into our world in a way which builds her confidence.

There are some superb teachers and advocates of force-free dog training, and you'll find those I am particularly indebted to in the Resources section at the end of this book. Some of the methods I'll be showing you are well-known in the force-free dog training community, while many have my own particular twist.

My work revolves around puppies, new rescue dogs, growly dogs - and, of course, dog owners. There are many people more gifted than I who can train animals to do astonishing things. My gift lies in being able to convey my knowledge to the dog's caregiver in a way which has them saying, "It's so obvious when you put it like that!"

Dogs are individuals and so are their owners, so sometimes creativity and imagination are needed to solve a problem. There isn't a one-size-fits-all approach to training - as you'll see when you look at the Troubleshooting sections following the lessons in the book.

I suggest you read the whole book before you start so you yourself are clear what you need and what you are aiming for. Then re-read the lesson you're working on and go straight into your very short session. After this you can assess where you are and check the Troubleshooting section for any difficulties that relate to you and your dog. Then you're ready for your next session the next day.

Chapter 1
It's all about choice

Lacy's self-control is sorely tested!

Wouldn't you like your dog to make the right choice without having to be told every time? This is how we bring up children. Take toothbrushing, for example. To begin, we have to brush our children's teeth for them, then we move to telling them to do it. As they get a bit older, we ask them if they've remembered to do it. Eventually (I see wry smiles from the parents amongst you!) we stop altogether and they do it by themselves.

This is what we are aiming to accomplish with your dog.

Dogs are simple souls. They do what works. They operate entirely on consequences. For instance, if they get lots of tasty morsels when they raid the bin, they'll do it again. If they raid the bin and get their head stuck and cut their tongue on a tin, then they may not attempt it again! If they raid the bin and it's empty - or full of non-food items - they'll probably try again another time. If they've successfully raided the bin before, and this time it's empty, then they'll keep trying until they get something - or till they're satisfied that the bin is always empty.

This is a bit like us with a one-armed bandit: people don't leave after a payout. They keep trying till they run out of money then leave, dispirited.

Your dog is making choices all the time. We just want to direct her to make the choices we like.

What will this mean for your dog?

- No more mysterious tellings-off for breaking rules she didn't know existed
- More freedom!
- More companionship with you around the house
- More outings with you
- More affection and appreciation from you

What will this mean for you?

- No more shouting
- No barking commands which your dog doesn't understand
- No firefighting - trying too late to change something your dog is doing
- The comfort of trust
- Companionship (why did you get your dog in the first place?)
- Peace and harmony in the home

Choices, choices

In training, the simplest way to get the dog to choose is by – you've guessed it! - offering her a choice. This may appear totally obvious when you think about it, but if you go the other way, and continually limit her choices, she'll never learn what you want to teach her.

Sometimes it doesn't matter to you which she chooses, like when you ask her, "Do you want to play with your ball or your frisbee?" Sometimes it matters a lot, and you'll weight the choices so she's most likely to choose what you want.

Here's a quick example of weighting the choices, you offer to put her lead on. If she sits, you put it on. If she jumps about crazily, you put it away again. There isn't any need for shouting or dancing about! Both of those actions are going to wind up your dog as well as you, and are not going to achieve the outcome you want. It will lead to frustration all round and a breakdown in communication between the two of you.

Give your dog a choice, and *wait* for her to choose what action to take.

In the example of you offering her lead, the reward for sitting still to have the lead put on is going out for a walk. If she leaps about and yodels, you can simply and silently put the lead back where it lives, then sit down and read a book.

After a bit of puzzlement your dog will probably come and stare at you. She's trying to work this out. When you're ready, you can fetch the lead again. Hold it in front of you and *wait*. Is your dog a little calmer this time round? No? Put the lead away and go back to your book. Let the dog settle down.

Now try again. Hold the lead and *wait.*

By now your dog should have worked out that what she was doing before was not working, and she's ready to try something different. As soon as she stands still for a moment (a Sit is not necessary at this stage) and is quiet, you can tell her how good she is, put the lead on, and head out for the walk. You can gradually wait for a sit, a silent sit, a silent still sit, a silent still sit for the time it takes you to get your coat on, and so on, until the sight of the lead causes your dog to sit and wait patiently for the inevitable walk.

But before she can do that, she has to know that what *she* does affects what *you* do.

If you don't give her a choice it'll be pot luck whether she ever works it out. Giving her a choice, showing her that her actions affect outcomes, gives her a responsibility that she will grow into. This will change your relationship for both of you. Rather than a master-robot relationship, you will have a friend-companion relationship. Much easier, much calmer, and much more fun!

Special equipment you'll need to teach Impulse Control

You'll be glad to know that there isn't any special equipment needed for these lessons! Just your usual dog-gear, though we'll have a quick look at what works best.

- A soft collar - fit it as loose as possible but without her being able to wriggle backwards and pull it over her ears. A soft webbing collar is good. I prefer one that is minutely adjustable and with a snap fastening. You can also use a buckle collar, though these are harder to adjust in the small increments needed for a puppy or small dog as you're stuck with the pre-defined holes.

- A 6-foot lead - one that is soft on your hands. If you need control when you're off-road, you can use a 15-foot soft long line.

- And if you want to use a harness, be sure that it's one you'd be comfortable in if you were wearing it!

Equipment you do NOT want to use

There is a lot of equipment on the market that is not suitable for the kind of interactions you are going to want with your dog. What I mean by that is any kind of aversive equipment - things that work by tightening, strangling, cutting, poking, shocking, and jabbing - and things that don't allow communication between the two of you.

In other words, don't use anything made of chain or spikes or operated with a battery. Also avoid extendable leads, bungee leads, and harnesses that operate by cutting up under the armpits.

How to reward your dog for her brilliant self-control

You will need to be able to reward your dog whenever she does something you like.

You'll need:

- A selection of toys your dog absolutely loves. Balls on ropes; soft tug toys made of fleece, sheepskin, or rabbit skin; and teddy bear-type toys - are all good.

- Mega-desirable treats! This means treats that your dog will sell her soul for, not dry kibble or pocket fluff as a rule. You can get some first-class commercial treats if you hunt carefully, but the best treats tend to be home-prepared, soft, slippery, flavoursome, smelly, and small.

The treats need to be very tasty - your dog has got to really want them! You don't want her chewing and chomping on a biscuit for so long that she forgets what she earnt it for! The treat needs to slip down quickly and make your dog think, "Wow! How can I get some more of that?" Your dog needs to know what you like and what does not cut it with you. Every time she does something you like, you can mark it by saying, "YES!" and giving her a treat.

Good treats

- Cheese
- Sausage
- Ham
- Chicken
- Frankfurter
- Salami
- Homemade sardine, tuna, or ham cookies
- Freeze-dried 100% meat treats
- Dehydrated liver, heart, lung, etc

…real food in other words. Ideally, they slip down quickly so your dog wants more. Cut them up into small, pea-size treats.

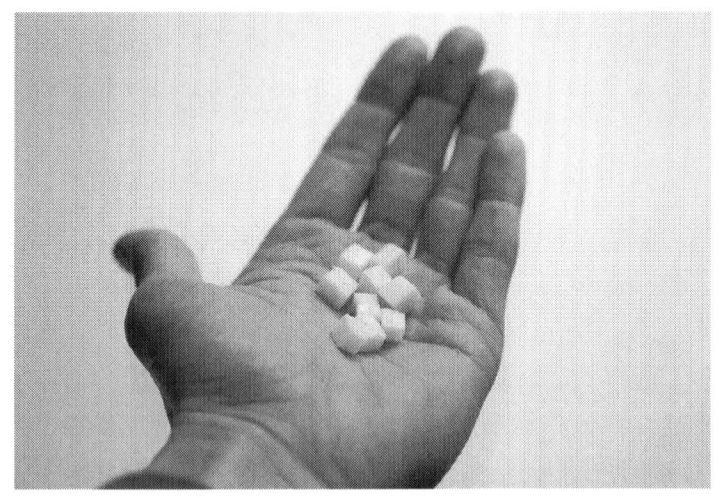

A handful of tasty little cheese treats

OK treats

- High-quality grain-free commercial treats

Fairly rubbish treats

- Your dog's usual kibble (She gets it anyway. Why should she have to work for it?)
- Cat biscuits
- Dog biscuits
- Stuff of unrecognisable composition sold as pet treats
- Anything you wouldn't put in your own mouth

Do you work more enthusiastically for £60 an hour or for 50p an hour? Quite so. Your dog is the same. Be sure the treats you're offering are worth working for.

Once you have these things in place, we're ready to get going with teaching your dog impulse control. You will probably be amazed at what your dog can do, and you will discover hitherto unknown depths to her personality. Let's get started!

In this Chapter we have established:

- Your dog needs to be given a choice to make a choice
- Your dog needs to be free to make mistakes and find out what works
- The importance of the right tools and the right treats
- "I like these new tasty treats! What do I have to do to get them?"

Chapter 2
Introducing the Magic Hand

Coco at 16 weeks admiring my lunch

You're going to teach your dog to control her impulses without shouting - or even speaking! You're going to work calmly and wait for her to figure out the game you're playing. Remember, your goal is to have her make a good choice all by herself.

Choose a quiet time, when you know your dog is hungry and not too tired. Prepare your treats and sit in a chair.

Lesson 1 Teaching the Magic Hand Game

1. Take a few of those tasty, flavourful, and strongly scented treats

2. Hold your hand out to your dog to show her what you have

3. As soon as she moves her nose forward to take the treats, close your fingers to hide the tasty snack

4. Keep your fist closed, fingers facing up, at dog-nose level. This is not a game of chase-the-hand, so keep your hand still. Now exercise your own impulse control by waiting.

5. Your dog will sniff, lick, poke, paw, and nuzzle at your hand. She may nibble your fingers. Let her.

6. If she really hurts you, you can say, "Ow", take your hand away for a moment, then put it back.

7. Carry on waiting while your dog pokes, sniffs, licks and nibbles. This will take as long as it takes - maybe several minutes for a determined thief.

8. At some stage she will stop digging at your fist. She will move her head away from your hand, and when she does, immediately open your fist to expose the food and close it again just as fast - before she dives in. Keep doing this every time she gives you a bit of space.

9. Your dog is discovering that moving away makes the hand open while being too close keeps the hand closed. Once she figures this new part of the game out, it's only a hop to discovering that staying away keeps the hand open!

10. Now watch your dog carefully. Dogs give different signs that they are waiting: some will lie down and stare at your hand, some will back away, some will sit and stare at you, some will turn their head right

away. Whatever sign your dog gives to show that she wants the food but that she's not going to try and snatch it, will take you to the next step. (If she just loses interest and wanders off, common in puppies, just make a kissy noise or touch her lightly to get her attention back to the task. We want distance, but we want her to stay engaged.)

11. While your dog keeps her polite distance, keep your cupped hand still, and slowly - with your other hand - take one treat and bring it towards her."Slowly" because we want to give her the chance to make a mistake. If she stays still, give her the treat, congratulating her warmly. If she lunges forward to meet it, drop it back in your hand, and close your fingers over it again. Just like us, dogs learn through their mistakes. Very soon she'll suss it out and stay rigidly still while you pass her a treat

12. Keep going with this sequence daily till your dog sees your fist in front of her nose and immediately backs off, sits, lies down, turns away, or gives whatever her sign is to show she's waiting. Once she gives the sign and stays still, you can slowly give her a treat with your other hand.

Many people are amazed the first time they run through this to find that their dog - however greedy she may usually be - can control herself and wait politely. Isn't this fun!

Impulse control is very much what we expect from our children, not to mention adults! When we put a plate of cakes on the table, we don't expect our visitors to dive on them and shovel them into their mouths. We expect them to wait patiently till we offer them a cake, then they put out their hand - without sticking their face in the plate - and take just one cake. You can expect the exact same manners from your dog.

Surprised?

Good! There are many more surprises on the way for you.

Troubleshooting

My dog tries for a while then wanders off.

Make sure your treats are highly desirable. I always like to know the treats I'm using are a personal favourite of whichever dog I'm working with. Remember, every dog is an individual. Choose a quiet time to start. Have her on a loose lead and tread or kneel on the lead to keep her from wandering too far. Persevere! It's important that you have impulse control and patience as well!

Ow! That hurts! My dog is scrabbling at my hand with his sharp claws!

Try holding your hand a little higher - right at nose level - to dissuade so much pawing. You can also clip and file his claws before your next session!

This seems to take forever.

Some dogs can take a while before they make the connection. Choose a quiet place to work. And keep going. Your dog needs to learn the consequence of her actions. We want her to know that she can get the treats when she cracks the code.

When I give her the treat from my hand she guzzles the whole lot.

Wait - you are picking up one treat and offering it with your other hand, right? Your dog never gets to put her nose in the treat-hand. She has to wait politely to be offered one treat, just like your visitor keeping a polite distance when offered the plate of cakes.

She seems to have got this, but when I tell her to sit she ignores me.

Don't tell her to sit - or anything else. We're looking for just one thing here: your dog controlling her natural impulse to grab any food in front of her. Telling her to sit is muddying the waters. You don't need to speak at all, though you can always tell your dog how brilliant she is, of course!

My dog doesn't seem to know what's wanted. He just sits there looking baffled.

Try to make the game more active, faster, and more exciting. You can also start off by giving him one of these amazing treats, so now he'll want to get more. As soon as he is not actively attacking your hand, you may open it so he can see the treats. Shut it fast. Open it. Shut it fast. If you have always told your dog what to do, or more likely what not to do, he may be waiting for direction from you. Stay silent, and let him see that he can make choices all on his own! We want the dog to try things, to see what works.

What do you mean by "engaged"?

Good question! I mean that your dog is totally involved in this game. She has bright eyes, cocked ears, swishing tail, and quick movements while she tries different ways to get the food. If she is "disengaged" she may be wandering off looking for something else to do, sniffing the floor, her movements slow. She may also be anxious as she's not sure what it is you want her to do. Anxiety will show up as yawning, avoiding eye contact, lip-licking, or lying down. If your dog is really worried and unhappy about playing with you, choose a better time and better treats, and encourage her attempts by using your voice. Don't make it easier or she won't learn anything! Make the game fun for your dog - it's a puzzle for her to solve.

My dog isn't that interested in food.

All dogs - indeed all animals - are interested in food. They have to have this drive or they'd die of starvation. So you need to set things up for success. Be sure your dog is hungry and has not eaten very recently. Get mega-super-incredible treats that smell intoxicating. A friend of mine calls them, "crack cocaine cookies"! The treats need to smell intoxicating to your dog, not to you - you may not be quite so enamoured of the smell of sardines or liver. If he's still not taking the treats, this indicates that he's too anxious and unsettled to work for you. Find out what's troubling him in the environment before you try again.

My dog is confused. I've been teaching her Hand Targets, so she thinks she should be bopping my hand with her nose!

Have a look at exactly what you do with your hand when you invite a Hand Target. Make sure your hand gestures are quite different for this game. You may, for instance, often be standing to teach Hand Targets, so you can sit and rest your arm on your knee for this lesson. Don't work them both in the same training session. Hand Targets are usually fairly active and fast. Your impulse control game will be quieter, more thoughtful. Be clear and your bright dog will work it out.

This seems too simple. As soon as she moves her face from my hand I give her a treat?

It is simple - yes! - but you've made it a bit too simple, and you're missing your greatest teaching opportunity. Once your dog pulls away from your closed hand, you open the hand. It's staying away from the treats in the open hand that's really hard! You need to wait for her to cue you that she is waiting. As soon as she's positively staying away you can then move to Step 11.

How on earth will this stop her chasing squirrels?

I'm glad you're thinking more broadly. Squirrels? That's food on the move. Once you've started to develop your dog's impulse control you'll be able to generalise it to other things. This will come later in the program. Get this part going first. We want to embed this in her subconscious so that the ability to resist becomes easy for her.

This last question is a useful segue into the next section:

How will this help with everyday grabbing and stealing?

To start with, we're focussing on food, which is the prime mover for most dogs and the easiest way to get very quick results. For now, you'll be able to proof your dog against

- Countersurfing - snaffling food off the kitchen worktops
- Cake on the coffee table
- Roast beef on the dinner table
- Sandwiches on the picnic rug
- Remains of the takeaway in the bin
- Dead rat in the hedge
- Biscuit in a child's hand
- Intercepting food on its way to your mouth
- Begging

We'll add a vocal cue to her action of turning away from temptation later on when she's doing it perfectly every time. For now you can use your Magic Hand to stop food attacks - there's no need to say anything. Instead of yelling, *"Oh no, the dog's about to eat the cake!"*, causing universal panic and rushing to grab the dog, simply put your hand in front of the desired object and wait silently.

Your dog - if well-schooled in the sequence you worked on in the first lesson, the Magic Hand - will say, "Oops. Oh yeah, not for me," and back off.

What do you do then? Tell her off for trying to attack the cake? Send her out of the room for being a "bad dog"? NO! *She made a good choice* (albeit with a little help from your Magic Hand). You reward her! "What a good girl! Here's a treat for you," is what you'll be saying. Now she remembers how she can earn rewards from you.

Life becomes simpler

As you can see, this process shifts the choice to your dog. We are no longer dealing with a robotic dog who needs to be directed and commanded every moment of the day. *Your dog is taking responsibility for her own actions.* Once she's able to make a choice, she is involved in the process, rather than being a victim. You'll be seeing in the following chapters how to achieve this happy state for everything you expect of your dog.

In this Chapter we have established:

- How to start to teach your dog impulse control
- Lots of everyday problems will evaporate
- Life will become much easier!
- "I get loads of cheese!"

Chapter 3
Keeping away from dropped or found food on the ground

Oops! I dropped a waffle, but it's quite safe from Cricket without me having to say a word

By now you've been working the game in the last section for several days, and your dog knows the Magic Hand. When you offer your hand with treats in to her she says, "Ha! I know this game: you can't catch *me*!" This is the playful attitude you should be aiming for. This is a game. This isn't a way of stopping your dog doing something. It's a way of involving your dog in your life and allowing her to make a choice. All you have to do is be patient and ready with a handsome reward for the right decision.

Making the right choice will become more rewarding to your dog than scarfing up the food she's found.

That's been scientifically proven. Finding food will become an opportunity for her to perform her party trick, and gain a reward plus your pleasure and attention. Locating food will trigger the reward centres in the brain, even without getting the food.

Now we're going to move the game forward and look at teaching your dog to leave food on the floor.

This will include:

- Dropped food
- Found food
- Plate or cup on the floor in the living room
- Stolen food (if you weren't watching!)
- Disgusting yucky dead thing found on a walk - which will end up regurgitated on your bed
- Disgusting leftovers in town from last night's street carousing - resulting in more carpet-cleaning
- Dangerous substances or objects on the street
- Slugs, snails, pebbles, rubber bands
- Spilt chips outside the takeaway shop
- Something so rank that your dog can't decide whether to eat it or roll in it

The principle of this game is the same as in the first game - it's all about waiting for your dog to work the problem out and show self-control, without us telling her to do anything. But there is one major difference when working with food on the floor.

I never let my dogs have the food that they're keeping away from.

Once my dogs see anything on the ground, it's history. I will reward them for leaving it, but they'll never get it.

Many people teach their dog a sequence of "leave it - geddit!" with food on the floor. Dogs are great at anticipation - think of the sheepdog who sees one ewe twitch her ear in the wrong direction and he's round the outside of her like a shot, to herd her back in before she's been able to escape the flock. The Leave it - Geddit sequence will naturally become shorter and shorter, until your dog thinks, "I just have to stare at the food for a moment, then it's *mine, mwah-ha-ha!*"

Eating something found on the ground can have tragic results. The reason my dogs never get it is twofold:

1. Safety

- If I drop a bottle of pills - and the pills fly all over the place - I don't want my dog thinking he can just stare at them for a moment then start hoovering. Many of our over-the-counter medications are dangerous or deadly to dogs, never mind prescription drugs.
- It could be a packet of mince pies that has "fallen off" the kitchen counter, or perhaps someone's left the baking cupboard open and she's found the raisins - both are highly toxic to many dogs.
- Maybe you drop a box of chocolates or leave chocolate lying about. This too can land your dog in the vet's intensive care unit.
- You may come across some drug paraphernalia hidden on the street
- Slugs and snails can carry flukes and worms into your dog
- All told, what your dog finds on the ground is best left there

2. They can pass it by without demur

If they never get the thing they've located on the ground, then they won't bother looking for things on walks, and they won't expect you to do something with the found thing. Mine know that they get rewarded for pointing it out to me if I haven't spotted it myself. "Yes, it's a maggoty dead rat. Thank you for showing me - here's your treat." No need to haul your dog away from the prize. Life has just become a bit easier. Again.

Lesson 2 Teaching the Food-on-the-Floor Game, or Magic Hand 2.0

Once your dog has mastered the first Magic Hand Game, teaching this one is simplicity itself.

1. Take just two of those tasty, flavourful, and strongly scented treats, holding one in each hand.

2. Hold one hand out to your dog to show her what you have, then whap the treat onto the floor right in front of her, instantly covering it with your Magic Hand.

3. Keeping your hand still, palm down, you now exercise your own impulse control again by waiting.

4. Your dog will sniff, nuzzle and paw at your hand. Let her.

5. At some stage she will move away from your hand. Immediately lift your hand to expose the food, then slam it down over the tasty treat again just as fast - before she dives in. Keep doing this every time she gives you a bit of space. Huzzah! Your dog has just discovered that moving away makes the hand lift - it's the same game!

6. "I know this game!" She'll take up her accustomed position - backing off, lying down, staring at the food, sitting staring at you, turning her head away, or whatever she does with the Magic Hand Game - most importantly, she waits, tail wagging madly, while the defenceless treat lies on the floor in front of her.

7. Scoop up the first treat and give her the one from your other hand

with jubilation and enthusiasm for her cleverness.

8. Work on this game frequently, for just one cycle. You can gradually develop the game so that you can leave the first treat on the floor when she backs off, while you give her the second from your other hand. Then remove the first treat.

Troubleshooting

Ow! My dog is scrabbling at the back of my hand with her claws!

If you've worked sufficiently through the Magic Hand Game you shouldn't be getting scrabbling or scratching now. Go back and consolidate the first game so that she pulls away from your fist immediately, without nagging or mugging it.

This won't work for me: I toss treats on the floor in training.

So do I! It's a great way to get active training games going with your dog and to re-position them. They know the difference. I use a marker word before treating, so they know the tossed treat is for them, and the food is thrown within the context of a game we're playing. In the Food-on-the-Floor Game and Magic Hand Game you are offering your dog a choice. She needs to make the decision whether this food is for her or not. Mistakes are good, but confusion is not! Make sure your set-up is different and deliberate while she learns - possibly in a different part of the house.

My dog's backing off but only a little. When I lift my hand, her nose is only an inch from the treat, so she grabs it.

Wait her out. When she backs off a smidgin, uncover the food and cover it again fast! Speed is essential in this game. After a few times she'll realise that her nose is in danger, and that this is not working, so she'll back up a bit more. When she's drawn herself back to a polite distance that allows you to expose the treat without risk of it being scarfed up, you can give her your other treat.

My puppy lies down, so she's right on the treat.

When you first start this game your puppy may lie down by walking her front legs forward so she ends up too close to the treat. Just slide your hand-and-treat combo a little further away and continue the game. We're aiming for success, and if her nose is too close, it will be very hard for her.

Lesson 3 Bringing the game to real life!

Got Magic Hand 2.0 going well? Excellent! Now we can take it further and proof your dog against all things on the ground. Don't worry if your dog's toys are usually on the floor - we'll come to toys later. She can still play with them!

1. Drop a treat near your foot - be ready to cover it with your foot if your dog dives for it. This is the same gig - cover, uncover, cover, uncover - till your dog backs off, when you remove the treat on the ground and reward her with the treat in your other hand.

2. Put some food on the edge of a chair seat. Cover, uncover … You got it!

3. Put a treat on your knee. Cover, uncover … dog backs off … reward.

Once she's got this, you can develop this into real life. You're eating a sandwich, and you "drop" a bit of bread on your knee. If your dog is staring at you eating this is a good time to teach her not to beg. Cover the bread quickly before she can lunge forward to snatch it. Uncover, cover, uncover till she backs off. Now you can remove the bread and carry on eating your sandwich. Do I reward her? Nope. If I do I'll be encouraging her staring and begging. *She needs to learn that staring at someone eating is never going to result in a reward.*

What I *will* do is some more Magic Hand training a bit later, when I'm not eating. Then she'll be well rewarded for leaving the food.

Science has proven that the cue (what kicks off the behaviour) becomes a reward in itself. As with any training, you start with massive and frequent rewards, then gradually lessen the number of rewards till what you're rewarding becomes a normal response. This may take hours, days, weeks, or even months, depending on the strength of your dog's begging and stealing, and the consistency with which you work. If she's been doing it for years, then it may take a little longer than with a young puppy. Remember, practice makes perfect! – with bad habits as well as good ones. All dogs are individuals with different learning speeds and experiences.

Consistency and clarity are the keys.

The more thorough you are at teaching this, the faster it will work and the faster you can assimilate it into daily life. You can start doing carefully-monitored set-ups similar to those in Lesson 3 Bringing the game to real life. You can leave a bit of food on the table where your dog can clearly see it, then busy yourself with something else in the room while keeping a close eye on proceedings.

If your dog stares at the food, you can go over and place your hand in front of it to protect it while your dog readjusts her mindset and changes her position, leaving the food alone.

If, while you're away from her, she makes a move to the food, try and resist the temptation to yell, "Ah-ah," "Noooo," or any of those other knee-jerk reactions you no longer need. Remember your own impulse control. I would probably say "Oh?" in a quiet voice, possibly followed by, "Is that really what you should be doing?" I know my dog doesn't understand the words, but she understands the interruption. She will appreciate the reminder and wiggle up to me saying, "I wasn't really going to take it, honest!"

An important word about words

There will come a time when you won't need to say or do anything. You can leave food wherever you want - a plate of hot dinner on the table, cakes on the coffee table, sandwiches on the picnic table - and it won't be touched. I habitually put my meal on the coffee table then go to fetch a glass of water. There are four dogs milling around, but I know my food will be untouched. Leaving food alone will become your dog's default behaviour.

But a vocal cue is useful - to remind your dog of impulse control when she comes across an unexpected bounty on the ground, or to suggest a calmer behaviour when she sees something exciting like a ball being kicked by some kids in the park.

So how do you connect your chosen word or words to your dog's action? Not having verbal language, your dog doesn't learn words in the same way we do. She learns by association. You describe what the dog is doing with your chosen word - your word is a label for that action. When you pair your puppy's name with a treat every time she responds, she knows that sound always means to come to you for good things. You are labelling the action of turning towards you and coming to you as "Millie!" Now you've got attention and the beginnings of a rock-solid recall.

How do we name this pulling away from a desired object? We do it by simply labelling that action just as she's doing it, and here's how.

Up to now you've been letting your Magic Hand do the talking, but when your dog's really good at this game you can start adding the cue. You can, of course, use any word or words you like - there are no rules! "Leave it" is a commonly used cue, but sadly it's often said in a menacing or furious manner - usually far too late - when the dog already has her jaws wrapped around whatever it is her owner wants her to leave. In other words, the poor dog has never been taught any of this and her owner expects her somehow to just know.

I use "Leave it," as you'll see in the following lesson. You can substitute whatever word you want, or use "Leave it". If you do, you must promise me that you won't turn into a hairy snarling monster when you say it! You say it calmly and quietly - as you would say Sit, Down, or Good Morning - you say it happily - as you would say "Millie!"

As with any word you use to ask your dog to do something, *you only say it once*. Repetition produces the opposite effect from what you want - it reduces responsiveness.

Lesson 4 Adding the cue

1. Start your Magic Hand game with your dog.

2. When she's backing off into her usual position every time, saying, "Ha! You can't catch me out," quietly add the words "Leave it" as she is making her move away.

3. Reward.

4. Repeat 2 and 3 till she's paired "Leave it" with her action of moving away.

5. Start saying, "Leave it" just before you expose the food.

6. When you can say, "Leave it," and get the thoughtful backing-off even without any temptation being visible, you'll know you've taught the cue right.

Troubleshooting

I'm guilty of yelling "Leave it!" Is my dog doomed now?

The joy of this way of working is that you always start from where you are and progress forward. What happened previously is of little importance. You may like to consider finding a new word, especially if you find yourself unable to say, "Leave it" nicely. You could even go so far as to use "No," as long as it's a conversational and lighthearted "Ooh no!" as opposed to a finger-wagging, bend-over-and-scowl, "Noooooooooo!" If you do use "Leave it", be sure not to yell.

Lacy's Find

Here's a nice story for you, so you can see what you can expect!

I was playing with Lacy one day on a walk, throwing her frisbee for her - a quick game of speedy retrieves and returns to hand. As she was running back to me, a strong smell caught her by the nose. She stopped dead about 40 feet away from me, dropped her toy, and scooped something up from the ground. She tossed it in the air and caught it again. I called her as she picked *The Thing* up. I thought, "Well, she's swallowed whatever that was!" Leaving her beloved frisbee, she carried on running back to me and delivered to my hand a heap of fried chicken carcass discarded by a thoughtless picnicker. She hadn't eaten her find! She ran off again for her toy, I bagged and pocketed the bones, and we carried on playing.

Real-life Magic Hand at a distance.

In this section we have established:

- How to keep dropped or found food left where it is
- The safety advantages of this game
- Walks will become less stressful
- Words are not necessarily necessary
- "I prefer Mum's approval and a smidgin of hot dog to squashed chips on the road."

Chapter 4
Why does it work?

If facts and figures are anathema to you, skip to the next section. But if the nuts and bolts of human and animal behaviour interest you - why we actually do what we do - then read on.

People first

There is plenty of scientific proof concerning the principles of instant *versus* delayed gratification in humans, and it appears to me that it works just the same in your dog.

Sigmund Freud, back in 1911, argued that deferred gratification was a marker of increased maturity. Then Walter Mischel conducted his Marshmallow Test experiments at Stanford University in the late 1960s, on children between ages 3 and 5. In the Marshmallow Test, a child had to choose between eating one favourite treat straight away, or - if they could wait for 15 minutes - be rewarded with two treats. A small number of the children caved in straight away and settled for one treat. Of the remainder who chose to wait, only one third managed to last out the fifteen minutes and earn their double reward.

One of the findings was that if the researcher interacting with the child appeared inconsistent and broke promises, the child would lose faith in the new game and just take his one marshmallow while he could. This provides an interesting insight into our need as parents and dog-owners to be consistent and reliable - however busy or stressed we may be!

The detailed follow-up studies over the next 40 years were revealing. The children who, at 4, were able to delay gratification did better in school and university, were more successful, and enjoyed a more healthy lifestyle. The ability to make good choices is a predictor of a person's ability to make the best of their life. They can choose rational behaviour over desires - the pre-frontal cortex over the limbic system.

Cognitive Behavioural Therapy uses the "if-then" framework to help people overcome unwanted desires. "If this happens, then I move into that strategy." Repetition leads to new habits being formed.

Moving into specifically dog-focussed scientific work, the two pillars are Pavlov, the originator of Classical Conditioning, and B.F. Skinner, whose pioneering work with a broad range of animals resulted in Operant Conditioning being shown to be the best way to train any animal. We're animals too.

Pavlov's Dogs and Classical Conditioning

Classical Conditioning was first described by Ivan Pavlov (1849-1936). This area of study came as a by-product of his pioneering work on the digestive system for which he won a Nobel Prize in 1904. His work was far-reaching and forms the basis of what we know about digestion today.

But his name has been linked in the popular mind with one thing only – *Pavlov's Dogs*. In his study of the purpose and function of saliva, Pavlov used dogs in his laboratory. They were kept immobile, with drains collecting the saliva through fistulae in the dogs' necks. The objective was to collect the saliva for analysis when the dogs were fed. It was soon discovered, however, that the dogs would begin salivating increasingly earlier in the food preparation chain - first the sight of the lab technicians, then the sound of human activity, became enough to get the juices flowing in anticipation of their food.

Pavlov's genius was in interrupting this chain with a specific, non-food-linked sound. Amongst others, he chose his famous bell. The bell was rung before feeding, and after a few exposures, the dogs would begin to salivate at the sound of the bell - regardless of the time or other factors – and in the absence of food. Pavlov had effectively put the salivation (an unconditioned or spontaneous, unconsidered response) under stimulus control. Put another way, the bell cued the drooling. So by using a hitherto neutral stimulus (the bell) he could cause the salivation to occur without the normal, natural, unconditioned stimulus of the presence of food. The association that the bell signified food meant the bell would cue the drooling in the absence of food.

How does this apply to us?

With your own dog, you'll be able to see many examples of Classical Conditioning at work.

- Barking at the doorbell
- Leaping up at the sound of the car keys or when seeing you pick up the lead
- Appearing at your feet when you bang the dog bowl
- Rapt attention at the sound of the fridge door opening,
- or a plastic bag rustling,
- or the cat flap opening!

These sights or sounds all stimulate a response of excitement or salivation, even without the expected result of a visitor at the door, going for a walk, dinner, or the entry of the cat. This response has developed through continual repetition of a sequence which the dog anticipates.

You can see now where some of your dog's more annoying habits have come from, and how you can change them! Control the stimulus (the thing that's causing the reaction) and you control the outcome. In fact, if you remove the stimulus entirely - disconnect the doorbell, for instance - you can completely eliminate that response. Think about that!

Operant Conditioning

Operant Conditioning is the name given to the shaping system first described by B.F. Skinner (1904-1990) in 1938 in *The Behavior of Organisms*.

Skinner was influenced by Pavlov. Working largely with rats and pigeons, Skinner's work had a far-reaching effect on education and psychology. From a practical standpoint, it was used extensively in the American war effort in the forties. Dolphins were used for underwater work where it was unsafe for divers, and chickens became ace spotters - of life rafts in a choppy ocean far below the rescue plane - and of bombing targets.

It was developed and refined by the dolphin trainers who, after World War II, turned their attention to training animals for aquarium displays. The dolphin trainers introduced a marker. It's impossible to get a fish to a dolphin at the high point of a jump, so they marked the moment with a whistle, signalling the correct response from the animal and the imminent arrival of a fish. This whistle is a Secondary Reinforcer.

- A Primary Reinforcer is something that the subject finds innately reinforcing, such as food, play, or social interaction.

- A Secondary Reinforcer is found rewarding by the subject by its association with a Primary Reinforcer, for example money, tokens, whistle, clicker, or a marker word - "Yes!"

Operant Conditioning is so called because the subject has to decide to do something to achieve a reward - to operate on its environment. In Classical Conditioning, an action which occurs naturally is paired with a stimulus or cue. For example, offering your hand for the dog to touch: the dog comes to sniff your hand, then you add the cue. In Operant Conditioning the animal can make a choice of what behaviour to offer.

In a Skinner box - a small chamber for testing the responses of animals, often equipped with a food-producing mechanism - rats or pigeons could sleep, groom, run around, or press a lever which delivered food - a Primary Reinforcer. Skinner introduced Pavlov's discoveries by pairing a stimulus to the food delivery, so the subjects knew that touching the lever produced food. Naturally, touching the lever became very popular! When Skinner stopped rewarding the lever-pressing by failing to deliver food, after a flurry of repeated attempts and frustration the action died out entirely - an Extinction Burst.

Why does this matter to me and my pet dog?

The possibilities opened up by Operant Conditioning extend far beyond simply achieving a desired action. It has become a window into the animal's mind. Daily, we are extending our knowledge of how the critters think. The practical applications are boundless: in dogs alone we have mine detection, search and rescue, dogs for the disabled, hearing dogs for the deaf, seeing dogs for the blind, seizure alert medical assistance dogs, companion dogs, entertaining dogs, dancing dogs, agility dogs. A lot of the things these dogs can do would be very difficult, if not impossible, to teach by force, by luring, or by moulding the action - and there would be no enthusiasm and joy in the task!

Skinner's pioneering work, followed up and expanded by Marion Breland, Bob Bailey, and Karen Pryor amongst others, has enabled dogs to be used in so many of these new applications.

The important thing to remember with Operant Conditioning is that what you reinforce is what you get, so the timing of the reward is crucial! One moment you think you are capturing a wonderful Sit Pretty, but because you were too slow with the reward, you actually reinforced a floppy Sit. Remember the dolphins jumping: your marker means a reward. Clarity is key!

A word about punishment

Operant Conditioning has its own clearly defined language - Reinforcement or Punishment, Positive or Negative - which may not mean the same as is popularly perceived.

- Positive means adding or starting something
- Negative means taking something away or stopping it
- Reinforcement means to encourage what you want by rewarding it, making it more likely to happen again
- Punishment refers to punishing the behaviour, not the animal, making the action less likely to happen again. It does not necessarily include traditional punishments such as beating.

Put very briefly:

- Positive Reinforcement = Good starts
- Positive Punishment = Bad starts
- Negative Reinforcement = Bad stops
- Negative Punishment = Good stops

You don't need to remember all this - *just aim for Positive Reinforcement and reward what you like!*

If your dog does something you like, for instance, and you turn away and ignore her, this is punishing - discouraging the action. Imagine walking down the street, spotting someone you know, giving a cheery smile, and your acquaintance turns his head sharply away to walk past you without a word. How would you feel? What would you do next time you saw him on the street?

Skinner proved that if an action is rewarded, the subject is likely to repeat that action. Similarly, if an action is punished, the subject is unlikely to repeat it. How many times did you have to put your hand into the steam from a kettle before you stopped doing it? There is fallout from punishment, however, that eliminates its use from any humane training program. Obviously it causes unhappiness and pain, which should render it unacceptable to civilised people, but it also causes distrust, alienation, lying, and deceitful behaviour. If a child has been smacked for stealing a cake, he's going to make very sure he doesn't get caught while stealing the next one! It doesn't necessarily stop what you don't want - it may drive it underground.

Repeatedly rewarding what you do like will work much, much faster, and your dog's response will be durable - she'll always make the right choice. It is the element of choice that will transform your relationship with your dog, and - secret tip! - it works just the same with children, spouses, and work colleagues!

Think of the joy of never administering a telling-off ever again.

In this Chapter you've learnt that:

- People and dogs are much the same
- The research into the dog's mind is very advanced
- How you can adapt this knowledge for you and your pet
- "It's all Greek to me."

Chapter 5
Here comes the joy!

Rollo waits in front of the open door for permission to go out

The spin-off from teaching your dog impulse control with food can now be extended to impulse control with everything else. Here are twelve things for you to enjoy working on.

1. The Door

When you head to a door, do you get run over by a stampede as your dog crashes past your legs, bolting through the door as soon as it's opened a crack?

Let's change this, straight away:

1. Using the calm response you have taught with the Magic Hand Game, you head to the door and put your hand on the handle.

2. As your dog skids to a slippery halt and thuds into the closed door you ask for a Sit - only once. If you worked through the first book in this series Calm Down! Step-by-Step to a Calm, Relaxed, and Brilliant Family Dog you'll know that you can use your mat to help you here.

3. Once she sits, remove your hand from the door handle and toss a reward behind her so that she's up again.

4. Repeat, until your hand on the door handle causes her to sit without you needing to say it. This may take one or several short sessions depending on how good your timing is.

5. Once she sits every time you touch the door handle, you can start to turn the handle, but only as long as she stays sitting. Toss the treat away. If she jumps up, go back to Step 4.

6. Gradually your dog will learn to wait while you actually turn the handle without moving the door, then open the door a crack - this stage may take a while. But when you can open it a crack, keep working till you can open it fully while she sits - and waits. Huzzah!

7. Say your release word to send your dog through the door. You have got a release word, haven't you? I use "Break".

8. Advanced stuff: as she goes through the door, say Sit and she will turn, sit, and wait for you to come through, shut the door, and lock it.

2. The Car Door

Your dog will wait seated to get in the car, and - importantly for safety - she will wait till you "break" her to get out of the car, then sit beside you while you close the door and lock it.

LEAVE IT!

1. Using the calm response you have taught with the Magic Hand, you head to the car with your dog on lead, and put your hand on the handle.

2. As your dog dances about waiting to hop in, you ask for a Sit - once. If you worked through the first book in this series, *Calm Down! Step-by-Step to a Calm, Relaxed, and Brilliant Family Dog,* you'll know that you can use your mat to help you here.

3. Once she sits remove your hand from the car door handle and toss a reward behind her so that she's up again.

4. Repeat, until your hand on the car door handle causes her to sit without you needing to say it. This may take one or several short sessions depending on how good your timing is.

5. Once she sits every time you touch the door handle, you can start to operate the handle. As long as she stays sitting, toss the treat away. If she jumps up, go back to Step 4.

6. Gradually your dog will learn to wait while you actually make that door-opening clunk with the handle without moving the door, then open the door a crack. As before, this stage may take a while, but keep working until you can open the door *fully* while she sits - and waits. Huzzah!

7. Say your release word to hop your dog up into the car. You have got a release word, haven't you? I use "Break."

8. Use the exact same sequence for releasing your dog from the car. You'll need to have her in a crate or you can lean in a side door to tether her so you don't slam the door on her head if she anticipates her release word.

9. You will be reaching in to clip a lead to her collar before releasing her, unhitching the fixed lead if you just tethered her. You may do

this several times in the sequence (clip on, clip off) so that she learns this is one of the stages she has to wait for.

10. Advanced stuff: Say "Sit" as she hops out of the car so she can spin round and sit beside you while you lock up the car.

3. The Crate

Does your dog have a crate or playpen? Use the same process for exit from the crate. Your hand on the crate latch will cause her to sit, then wait when the door is open till she's invited out to sit beside you.

1. Using the calm response you have taught with the Magic Hand, you head to the crate and put your hand on the latch.

2. Your snoozing dog will jump to attention. Open the crate door a crack, whoosh your arm in and give her a reward while sitting. Hold the treat up over her head so she has to be sitting to reach it. Shut the door and latch it again.

3. Repeat straight away until your hand on the door latch causes her to sit without you ever needing to say it. This may take one or several short sessions depending on how good your timing is.

4. Once she sits every time you touch the door latch, you can start to open the crate door a crack. As long as she stays sitting, give her a treat. If she jumps up or tries to bolt out of the crate, just close the door gently and go back to Step 3.

5. Gradually your dog will learn to wait while you open the door more widely. This stage may take a while, but continue to work until you can open it *fully* while she sits and waits. Huzzah!

6. Say your release word to let your dog come out of the crate. You have got a release word, haven't you? I use "Break".

7. Advanced stuff: as she comes through the door, say, "Sit," and she will turn, sit, and wait beside you - instead of hurtling off to follow her own agenda.

4. Furniture

How about hopping up on the furniture?

Maybe you let your dogs snooze in an armchair, or sit on your lap while you relax - I do - but that doesn't mean you have to put up with being landed on when you have a bowl of soup on your lap! And it certainly doesn't mean that you may not sit in your own armchair because your dog is in it.

Using the same system of impulse control, my dogs will sit beside me and "ask" to get on my lap. If I want that, I'll invite them to hop up. It took no time for my puppy to realise that leaping up unbidden resulted in landing on the floor again, while sitting patiently got him the cuddle he wanted.

The Magic Hand system taught him that nagging doesn't work, while patient waiting at a polite distance does.

1. Your dog is about to leap onto your lap.

2. Hold up your hand like a policeman.

3. Ask her calmly, "What do you think you should do now?" Remember that interacting with your dog does not need to include yelling, "Gerroff! SIT!"

4. *Wait* for her to give an appropriate response. The first time out it may be just to stand and wait. You can reward this stage by inviting her up.

5. Next time you can *wait* for her to give you a Sit before inviting her up.

My dogs are welcome to use my chair when I'm not in it, as long as they hop off as I approach it.

1. Dog is snoozing in your chair - that's fine - but you want to sit there.

2. Move purposefully towards the chair.

3. Dog stays put.

4. Lower yourself carefully into the chair and slowly lean back.

5. By now your dog will have hopped off.

6. In future, just advancing on the chair will be enough to let your dog know she should move.

Serious note: If you get any growling or nastiness, this is indicative of a larger problem of Resource Guarding and you need to find a force-free trainer straight away to help you. Do not get bitten!

5. Toy Play

Playing tug is a great way to teach your puppy Impulse Control

Playing exciting games with your dog is the key to building a terrific partnership, but just like our games, games with your dog need structure and boundaries.

Playing tennis with a friend would be no fun if he insisted on standing on the same side of the net as you, or simply hit all the balls over the fence. All our games have rules and structure. So you decide on the rules of play with your dog. Basically my rules are simple: my dog should not snatch the toy from my hand, grab my sleeve, or leap up and bite my nose; she should give the toy up when I want it back, and she should not dodge about just out of reach.

Use your Magic Hand principle:

1. Hold out the toy. If she tries to grab it, the toy disappears behind your back until she waits calmly. When you bring it out, she continues to wait calmly till it's offered to her. If she tries to grab it, it goes back behind your back again. Run through this quickly.

2. When she's clearly not jumping it's Game On: you whack the toy on the floor or hold it out to her saying, "Geddit!"

3. To get the toy back, either put a treat to her nostrils or relax your pull on the toy and wait for her to let go - give the treat and start again; or, if she's pulling like a maniac and has no interest in the treat, *gently* hold her collar still so she can no longer pull while you relax your pull on the toy till she's so bored she lets go.

Either way, it's her choice to keep to these rules.

If your puppy is over the top, snatchy and bitey, she's probably too tired. She needs a break in her crate for a good sleep before the next game.

6. Reclaiming Stolen Shoes

Your dog has grabbed something you value and crouched into a playbow to invite you to chase her. Don't! If you do, you'll be playing her favourite game - forever.

1. Feign complete indifference about the article she has, get a tasty treat, offer it to her then close your hand over it. Magic Hand again. Now she's going to move into that state of mind which requires thinking in order to get the treat: "Ah! I know this game."

2. When she decides to wait politely, offer the treat to her with your other hand. She'll drop the precious item into your waiting hand so she can enjoy her treat. This can all be done without any shouting or histrionics from you.

3. Now get one of her own toys, chuck it for her, and enjoy a game.

4. And put your shoes away! Don't make life hard for yourself - or your puppy.

7. Mugging Your Hand or Your Pocket for Those Treats

Treat training can result in unwanted pestering or "mugging." Of course you'll never reward or reinforce mugging or begging by feeding your dog now, will you?

Mugging is the last thing we want, so encourage your dog to use her new-found impulse control to refrain from this practice.

1. Your dog is staring at your pocket, or nosing or nudging your hand for treats.

2. Turn so that your pocket is inaccessible, or clasp your treat-filled hands to your chest. Keep still and wait. This may be enough for her to realise her mistake and desist.

3. If necessary you can add, "What should you be doing right now?"

4. If neither of these is reaching your determined dog's mind, gently and silently slip your hand in her collar to lower her front feet to the ground - or hold her away from the pocket while she collects herself.

5. Tell her she's good and go about your business.

6. Soon you can ask her to do something and reward her. She needs to know that treats come as a result of doing something you like. It's up to her to work out what this may be!

7. Don't keep treats on your person. Have containers of treats strategically placed around the house so you can always catch and reward something good. They should be within easy reach - for you, but not for her!

8. Tasty Shopping Bags in the Car

1. Teach your dog that plastic bags are not fair game. You can do this in the kitchen.

2. Put the bag of goodies on the floor, quietly say, "Leave it," and reward your dog for leaving the bag of goodies alone.

3. Repeat a few times.

4. Now put the bag in the car and repeat.

5. Bags in the car will now earn the same respect.

Many years ago I had a small Whippet cross and a very large German Shepherd. Poppy had been leaving food bags in the car alone for years. When Corin, the huge young German Shepherd, went to stick his nose in a shopping bag, Poppy rumbled menacingly - thinking, "If anyone's going to get that food it'll be me!" Corin clearly decided that shopping bags were very dangerous, and forever after would plaster himself to the furthest part of the car when shopping bags were there. You can achieve the same effect with no growling!

9. Helping Tidy Up the Kitchen (aka Countersurfing)

Countersurfing is the annoying habit some dogs develop of cruising the kitchen worktops - either with two feet or all four! - scavenging any crumb, smear, chocolate cake, or rump steak that they may find.

First things first: if you don't want your dog to practice a bad habit then you must ensure that she has no opportunity to do so. So no food - crumbs count as food - may be left on the kitchen counters, and *never* leave her in the kitchen unattended.

Then use your Magic Hand.

1. Remember the food on the floor sequence? If your dog's nose appears in front of some food you're preparing, there's no need to yell or dance. Just put your hand in front of the food, giving her a moment to process this information - then she'll drop her feet to the floor again.

2. Reward her for a little distance and when she's not begging.

For an ongoing counter-countersurfing program, you can't beat Impulse Control combined with Matwork. Fortunately there's a book in this series, *Calm Down! Step-by-step to a Calm, Relaxed, and Brilliant Family Dog* - more info in the Resources section - which will take you step-by-step to having a calm and relaxed dog who goes to her mat and lies down whenever you start preparing food.

What about on walks?

10. Marking Every Tree

Not confined to males, this is often allowed to develop because people think it's a normal dog activity. Not really. My dogs can mark whatever they like on their own time, but if they're walking with me … they walk with me. In my mind, walking excludes hauling me towards every lamp-post to check the pee-mail. Allow your dog one opportunity to relieve herself. After that, she's walking with you. No marking.

Another book in this series - *Let's Go! Enjoy Companionable Walks with your Brilliant Family Dog* (info in the Resources Section) - will take you step-by-step to achieving calm and comfortable walks with your dog. Along with Impulse Control you have a winning combination!

But for now, you can engage your dog in conversation whenever a likely tree or lamp-post hoves into view. Congratulate her warmly for focussing on you as you walk blithely by. Remember always to reward anything she does that you like!

11. Passing Quietly By Previously Exciting Things

Your dog does not need to drag you excitedly towards every living being (or inert or dead thing) she sees on the street. Teaching her impulse control will spread into her everyday life so that she can view things more calmly and make better decisions.

If she's desperate to examine something, you can ask her for attention first, then give her permission to "Go sniff!" There's lots more about this in The Premack Principle which you'll find in a little while.

This system also leads to calm greetings when you want your dog to meet someone or another dog.

12. Meet and Greet Nicely

This is a large subject that I will only touch on here. If your dog is one of those that gets over-the-top excited at the sight of a person (heaven!) or another dog (wowee!!) - common in young sociable pups - you can help keep things calm by eliciting a bit of self-control before they are permitted to greet the object of their desire.

1. Wait for a Sit, or just eye contact, from your dog before giving permission to greet. I give permission by saying, "Go say Hi!"

2. You can interrupt the greeting by calling her back for a treat, then - if things are going well - she can greet again.

See *Let's Go! Enjoy Companionable Walks with your Brilliant Family Dog* for some cracking lead skills. Once you have these skills down, you never have to pull your dog's lead again. Really - never again!

The Premack Principle

This principle was first defined by the psychologist David Premack. For us, it simply means that your dog will choose to do something a bit dull or non-rewarding, such as sitting still in the face of temptation, in order to get something which is exciting and rewarding.

Think of a family situation where the children may watch television (very rewarding) as soon as they've put their things away (very, very boring). Kids will race with enthusiasm to bundle everything up and stuff it in a cupboard so they can get to their beloved tv. You can use the same principle with your dog, and it's all impulse control!

The greeting example in *12. Meet and Greet Nicely* above used Premack to teach your dog to choose to sit (boring) - difficult when she is desperate to bounce on a visitor - in order to get the release "Go say Hi!" (wonderful!)

Another way I use Premack to get nice walking on the lead from my pups is this:

1. You're walking your young dog and you come to a grassy area beside the path which screams, "Sniff me!"

2. Your pup lunges towards it, but you keep on walking by.

LEAVE IT!

3. When you've passed the spot, you can turn and walk back again.

4. Your pup lurches out again - keep walking.

5. After you've walked by the enticing grassy patch a few times, your dog will twig that she's not to pull you about and walk nicely with you.

6. The split second she does that, you can turn to the grass and say, "Go sniff!"

So she learns that walking nicely on the lead will buy her the opportunity to sniff exciting things.

Only do this once or twice on a walk with your young dog, otherwise she's going to think she can sniff every other blade of grass as long as she walks past with you first.

In this section we have established that:

- Impulse Control rules!
- You can apply this to many different areas of your daily life with your dog
- Your dog is so much cleverer than you thought!
- "I'm so much cleverer than you thought!"

Chapter 6
The effect of Impulse Control on the two of you

*The doughnuts are quite safe from Cricket the Whippet,
even without being reminded*

So how is this all going to affect your daily life with your dog?

What effect will this have on my dog?

First of all impulse control will give your dog a wonderful feeling of freedom. Impulse Control is empowering! In the same way that people "grow into" a senior role when promoted, you can watch your dog blossom as she learns to apply these principles to the whole of her life. Once you can trust her not to chew up the carpets or steal the sandwiches you can give her much more freedom. She can - in time - have the run of the house and garden without endangering the furniture, the fittings, the plants, the lawn, or any food left *anywhere*.

The trust you show in her will build her trust in you. Whenever she leaves anything tempting alone you must be sure to observe and reward her with whatever reward is suitable - from a smile or stroke to a treat or game. Her confidence will grow. She knows what she has to do and what is expected of her. *This clarity leads to self-confidence*. A dog who doesn't know what she's meant to do is forever looking over her shoulder wondering if she's going to be yelled at for some unknown transgression.

Your dog will become more patient, more thoughtful, and more reflective. This response will spread to every area of her life - and this response builds with experience.

In a multi-dog household new pups copy their elders. A useful spin-off is that your new puppy will now have excellent mentors to emulate and will learn much faster. Because there is a lack of confusion and your dog is clear on her boundaries, the general excitement level in the household is lowered. Instead of reacting to everything that occurs, your dog can take much more in her stride.

Will your dog pester you for food? No. She knows that begging and mugging is not rewarded. She knows she can earn rewards by pleasing you. This does depend on you being free with your praise and rewards - there's no place for miserliness here.

You make a deal with your dog: you do what I want and you'll get what you want.

Don't break that deal!

So how will all this affect me?

You don't have to keep everything you value under lock and key. You can take your lunch out to the garden and leave it on the picnic table – like the plate of doughnuts in the picture above - while you come back into the house for your drink or book. Instead of hairy sharks wheeling round the table waiting for their moment to strike, your dogs will pass no comment on this plate of goodies and it will be safe till you return.

If you take your dinner into the tv room, leaving it on the coffee table, it will still be there, untouched, when you come back. You can kick off your shoes and know that they will not be chewed or loved. If your young dog feels the need to chew, she knows where her toy box is and can help herself to one of her own chewies. Shopping bags with meat and cakes can be left on the floor waiting to be unpacked without wet noses rooting around in them. Like the bag containing the pork chops which was left on the floor by the fridge for hours the other day because of a distraction. The pork chops remained untouched all afternoon by the four dogs.

This is the same that we teach and expect of our children - only dogs learn way faster!

Your home is calmer. You are calmer. You trust your dog. You will be more patient - you too will learn impulse control! You'll know that shouting and frustration have no place in a mature relationship, and that just waiting for the desired response is enough. You honour your dog. You respect your dog. No longer is she a nuisance-mutt who needs to be restrained and whose base impulses need to be kept at bay.

Mutual trust

This mutual trust leads to a greater bond between you and your dog. Your companion can truly share her life with you. You know where you are with her. She can become the brilliant family dog you always wanted! When I put on my jumper there's likely to be a cascade of treats tumbling from the pocket and bouncing across the floor. Four dogs watch this with interest. Do they plunge in to hoover up the spilt treats as fast as possible? Nope. They wait. I clear up the dropped treats - but they each get one for their self-control and mature responsibility.

You've probably already been astonished by how quickly your dog learnt the Magic Hand trick.

I was working with an impulsive terrier who was in sore need of self-control. When I explained what I was about to teach him, his owners said, "That won't work for Dodger. He'll never give up trying to get the food out of your hand. He'll just keep on biting and digging." In a very short time - shorter than usual, in fact - their little dog was backing off politely from my hand to wait patiently for his reward. I think the owners' jaws are still dropped!

So how quickly can this spread to the rest of your dog's life? It really all depends - not on your dog - but on you. How consistent can you be? How calm and patient? How reliable are you? Remember the children in the Marshmallow Test who would not trust their researcher if he showed himself to be unreliable? If he couldn't keep a deal, why should they?

We only have our dogs for a short time - far too short. There is no time allowance for damaging and breaking your relationship. There is no point in trying to make a point.

Enjoy the simplicity of working with your dog on a choice and reward basis.

Life has just become so easy!

Side effects

And there's much more!

See this: once your dog has learnt to control herself around food, she can adapt this to controlling herself around other exciting things in her life -

squirrels, birds, other dogs, children running, balls, other dogs' toys, [*insert your dog's most exciting thing here!*]

You don't have to cover the other dogs or children with your hand! You appeal to the same reflective side of her nature to get her to think through a problem to figure out an appropriate reaction. Instead of the current, "SQUIRRELS!!!" and a full-speed hurtle towards them - deaf to your protests - you can get her to pause and think. If you like her calm response and the area is safe, you could consider sending her after the squirrels as a reward. Don't worry - the squirrels will always get away up the nearest tree! The thrill of speed and the chase is the reward.

So instead of the backing off signal, turning away her head, or whatever your dog was doing with the food in your hand or on the floor, you can ask for a Sit and eye contact before being given permission to greet a visitor, run towards another dog, chase a rabbit - or whatever it may be.

It may not be appropriate for the thing she wants to be a reward. So you'll have others up your sleeve - good treats or a favourite toy - so you can reward her for engaging with you, then keep that engagement as you move away from the distraction.

You are aiming for your dog to be able to respond to you when she's highly aroused by some deep instinctive drive. This is hard for her! It may take some time before she's able to do this - but she'll never be able to do it if you don't teach her.

Racing off impetuously can have tragic results, of course, if there happens to be a road between her and The Exciting Thing. It can also be a nuisance or cause trouble - knocking over a small child, for instance, or crashing into a dog that does not welcome attention.

You'll need a cast-iron recall too, see *Here Boy! Step-by-step to a Stunning Recall from your Brilliant Family Dog* - the fourth book in this series of Essential Skills for a Brilliant Family Dog. More information is available in the Resources section of this book.

Coco the miniature poodle pup adores people. He gets wildly excited at the sight of a new victim for his attentions. He sings, he dances, he pirouettes, and he waves his paws, but he's learning that no greeting will ever take place without quiet and stillness from him first. So the sight of an oncoming person is beginning to produce a Sit from him and a distracted gaze at me, with only very quiet squeaking while he waits for his permission to, "Go say Hi!" This will gradually improve until all the anticipatory noise is eliminated, and he can sit - genuinely calmly - in the presence of new people.

Remember in Chapter 5, *1. The Door* where your hand on the door handle produced a sit, resulting in the opening of the door? This is a similar game - only with far greater stimulation and distraction! The sight of The Desired Object is a cue for your dog to sit.

When I call my whippet Cricket off a bunny chase I can see the strong battle going on in her head, and I can see her joy when she makes a good choice. This is a result of strengthening her "decision-making muscles" in the face of the food temptation. Those muscles are now strong enough to resist the instinctive drive of a whippet to chase rabbits - what she was bred for.

If you can use impulse control to call a sighthound off a rabbit-chase - you're doing well! There is, of course, a strong recall here - more of that in *Here Boy! Step-by-step to a Stunning Recall from your Brilliant Family Dog* – the fourth book in this series.

That's mine!

Another area where Impulse Control can be of great help is that of Resource Guarding.

Resource Guarding is when your dog seriously guards something she values - usually by freezing, keeping her head low over the item, showing the whites of her eyes, wrinkling her lips, maybe snarling, growling, snapping, and if challenged, biting.

The thing she values could be food, a dead bird, a toy, a twig, a tissue, her bed, the car - or you. Or any number of other things she prizes.

If the Resource Guarding is *very, very mild,* opening and closing your Magic Hand in front of her can move her into that mental space where she stops reacting and starts thinking rationally. If this is the case, she can drop the item into your hand for you to admire and return to her, or to swap for a high-value similar object or a treat. Never try and snatch away the thing she's guarding.

You are not "climbing down" or "losing face." It's not about you. It's about changing your dog's perception of this attack on her in the most painless way possible - and the most effective way!

This will build her trust in you that you won't take away her prized thing, rather you'll reward her for letting you look at it and sometimes swap it for something else equally as good. Exchange is no robbery.

IMPORTANT WARNING: If the resource guarding is extreme or well established, and your dog is showing any of the signs in the list above, then you should not attempt anything at home, but immediately find yourself an experienced professional force-free trainer or behaviourist who will give you a program to safely manage then change this habit.

Never challenge a dog who is guarding something - you are likely to get bitten.

It's all tricks to them

20-week-old puppy Lulu waits patiently while I pile cheese onto her paws.

Let's move to an area where your dog's impulse control really comes into its own: Tricks! Combine impulse control with your dog's creativity and you'll both have great fun with them. There are some great tricks you can teach your dog which involve resisting temptation. People will marvel at what your clever dog can do! Remember that when teaching something you should focus on teaching and not testing.

Food on The Paws

Once you've gone through the steps of the Magic Hand with food on the floor in Chapter 3, Lesson 2, you're ready to teach your dog the trick of lying down with food on each paw - and leaving it alone!

1. You're covering and uncovering the food under your hand till your dog will give you her "Hallo, it's this zen thing again" action immediately, so you can reward her. Remember: She never gets the food that she's leaving; she gets food from your other hand.

2. Repeat Step 1 but gradually get your hand-and-food combo closer and closer to your dog's paws with each repetition until your hand is

touching her paw.

3. The next move will be to place the food on one of her paws and immediately cover it, uncover it, and so on.

4. When she's showing that she won't touch the food, you take it off her paw and offer her a treat from your other hand.

5. Once this one-paw trick is perfected, you can build this up to food on both paws.

6. And once your dog can do this trick for you in any room in the house you can try showing it off to your friends - who will be astonished!

Troubleshooting

My dog is doing this brilliantly till I put the food on her paw, then she snatches her foot away.

Some dogs have really tickly feet! Try handling her feet gently for a reward at other times in the day so she gets used to the sensation being a good thing. When you put the food on her paw use a firmer hand-touch and press the food gently onto her paw.

We were going great but she snatched the food up.

Don't take your hand away completely until you're sure she won't take the food. Also, keep it very quick to begin with. You can gradually add a little duration to this trick as you go along, but *don't leave your poor dog nailed to the floor by cheese cubes for long!*

Food on the Head

Once you've got the Food on the Paws trick perfected, you can go for an advanced trick. Keep in mind, this is harder for your dog because you have to get the food onto her head while she's trying to look up and see what you're doing with it!

1. Having her in a Down first may make this learning a bit easier.

2. You may need to get her focussing on the treats on her paws first so you can place the food on her head very, very gently without disturbing her.

3. Very carefully place a piece of cheese on her head. She may not even realise it's there - but it looks good!

4. Over time you can work on the head-food without the paw-food.

The Famous Tossing the Biscuit off the Nose Trick

You can build up to this trick. It's well-known, but surprisingly difficult for the dog. The trick involves placing a small biscuit, piece of cheese, or sausage on your dog's nose. She has to wait till you release her, then she can have it.

This will go through a few stages before you get the desired final trick.

1. You may have to ask your dog to place her chin on your palm so that her head stays level - otherwise the treats will be rolling off her nose all over the place!

2. When she's happy with that - don't forget to reward this new mini-trick! - you can hold the treat on her muzzle, just on the edge of the nose-leather is the best place. She'll go comically cross-eyed trying to look at it!

3. Remove that treat and give it to her.

4. She may still be resting her chin on your other hand, but slowly and gradually build up through the stages so that you can remove your

hand from the treat for a split second, then a second, then a little longer before you give her the treat. Eventually, remove your chin-support. Reward each step. Have fun with her!

5. Finally add your "Geddit!" cue so she can get the treat. She may well just tip her head so the treat falls on the floor. Enjoy her triumph and repeat the sequence on another day till she's really got it.

6. She'll start to pull her head away quickly and snatch the treat out of the air.

Have fun with this and you can impress your friends with her incredible Impulse Control!

In this Chapter we have established that:

- Having Impulse Control will change your dog's life
- It will also change your life
- You'll develop mutual trust
- A bit about Resource Guarding
- How to teach some great foodie tricks
- "I'm going cross-eyed staring at this cheese on my nose!"

Conclusion
You are a huge way into your journey!

If you've followed me through this book step by step, you'll now have a dog who can be trusted around food - whether found, dropped, or left out on a table or counter - and you'll be well on the way to having a dog who can contain her excitement in the face of her greatest challenges - children, people, other dogs, a moving ball or bike …

Or maybe you work like me and you've had a read-through first, so you know where you're going with this, and you're now ready to go back, read the book again and start the learning with your dog. There are just four skills you need to turn your wild puppy into your Brilliant Family Dog. Just four. Everything else flows from these. If you have these four skills - you're done!

You have in this book one quarter of what you need to have a Brilliant Family Dog. To find the other three parts, have a look at the Resources section at the end of this book.

Resources

If you've got any specific queries, you can email me direct at beverley@brilliantfamilydog.com This will come straight to my personal inbox and I'll answer you - usually within 48 hours. Try me!

Meanwhile, for more free training, go to www.brilliantfamilydog.com and get a series of instructional emails on common day-to-day problems, like jumping up, chewing, barking, and so on.

> Thank you for the insightful emails - we are applying the techniques and find the information really helpful. *Lucy and Ted*

> I just wanted to say how much I enjoy your emails. I nearly always learn something new and they also remind me of ways to encourage good behaviour and therefore promote everyday enjoyment for both my dogs and myself! *Amanda and Ella*

> Thank you for the emails, they are a great source of information. *Simon and Murphy*

> Thank you for all these brilliant tips! *Shabra and Archi*

> I've found your tips extremely interesting, helpful and above all really generous of you. Thank you. *Shelley and Jesse*

Works consulted for Chapter 4

http://www.britannica.com/biography/Sigmund-Freud accessed 2015

Mischel, W., et al. (1989). *Delay of gratification in children.* Science, 24 4 (4907), 933–938

https://www.apa.org/helpcenter/willpower-gratification.pdf accessed 2015

Casey, B. J., et al. (2011). *Behavioral and neural correlates of delay of gratification 40 years later.* Proceedings of the National Academy of Sciences, 10 8 (36), 14998–15003

http://www.nobelprize.org/nobel_prizes/medicine/laureates/1904/pavlov-bio.html accessed 2015

http://psychology.about.com/od/classicalconditioning/a/pavlovs-dogs.htm accessed 2015

Skinner, B.F. (1938) *The Behavior of Organisms: An Experimental Analysis*, New York; Appleton-Century

Skinner, B.F. (1951) *"How to teach animals"* Scientific American

Reynolds, G.S. (1968), *A Primer of Operant Conditioning.* Palo Alto, California: Scott, Foresman

Bailey, B, and M.B. Bailey (1996) *Patient Like the Chipmunks.* Eclectic Science Productions

http://www.clickertraining.com/karen accessed 2015

Mary R. Burch and Jon S. Bailey (1999), *How Dogs Learn*, Wiley, NY

Essential Skills for a Brilliant Family Dog

Book 3
Let's Go!

Enjoy Companionable Walks
with your Brilliant Family Dog

Beverley Courtney

Introduction
Oh no! Not again!

Don't walk behind me; I may not lead.
Don't walk in front of me; I may not follow.
Just walk beside me and be my friend.

- Anonymous

This walk is no fun!

You're ready for your daily walk. You are full of hope because you know today is going to be the day your dog walks nicely beside you without pulling your arm out of its socket. You are deluded. Yep, it's going to be just the same as usual.

Lead on = Carthorse mode.

She nearly pulls you over as you step over the threshold. She strains away from you while you try to lock the door. You reach the roadside, and it's head down, PULL! She's choking and spluttering, she's scrabbling along the pavement. She's lurching and weaving - this is no fun for either of you!

I know you've tried lots of gadgets and methods to try to make things better - things suggested by people in the park, by friends, family members, and even trainers - some against your better judgment. But why aren't any of them working? You've got collars and leads to beat the band - some of them designed to inflict pain or make holes in your dog's neck. These devices are sold to prevent pulling, but they just seem to encourage her to pull harder.

I'm guessing that you have been trying to teach your dog *not* to pull. This is sadly doomed to failure. If there's one thing dogs don't understand, it's *not* doing something.

Dogs are doers. They do things. They can't *not* do something. It makes no sense to them. What we have to do is show them something else to do *instead of pulling*.

Many people - and probably you too - have successfully taught their dog not to jump up for a treat by simply hanging on to the morsel until the dog is sitting. She can't jump and sit at the same time, so the jumping dies out.

We can use the exact same system for teaching your dog to walk nicely beside you on a loose lead. Like sitting when a treat is on offer, keeping the lead loose becomes the default behaviour for your dog when she's walking with you. She can't pull ahead and be by your leg at the same time, so the pulling dies out.

Really, yes! It will work for you too!

I've taught this system to hundreds of puppies and dogs, and I'm always amazed at how quickly the dog gets it - once the owner gets it!

You don't need any funny gadgets or kit - though I do have help for extreme *kamikaze* pullers - and there is no force, coercion, or intimidation involved. You're not telling your dog, "You'll do this because I say so." You're saying, "You do this because you like doing it."

You got a dog to be your companion, not to fight with. You wanted to enjoy the great outdoors. You wanted a reason to get out every day to meet people, to visit new places, to get fit, and maybe shift a few pounds.

None of this is going to happen if your walks are a tussle and a misery!

There is much more at stake here than just the health of your shoulders. You'll find endless reasons to put off a walk if it's such hard work. Not only will those pounds pile back on, but your dog will be under-stimulated and under-exercised - and that's a recipe for a dog looking for trouble!

It was having to learn the techniques to make a Brilliant Family Dog with my own busy household of multiple dogs, cats, sheep, goats, hens, and children that set me on the road to helping others do the same. I learnt early on that forcing someone to do something only resulted in grudging compliance at best; whereas getting them to participate and enjoy the process turned them into eager and fast learners. This applied equally to the dogs, the goats - and the children! The sheep and the cats not so much.

My qualifications range from the understanding of learning theory to specialist work for fearful, anxious, and growly dogs. Acquiring an anxious, growly dog of my own ensured that I learnt and understood the process of assimilating the dog into our world in a way which builds her confidence.

There are some superb teachers and advocates of force-free dog training, and you'll find those I am particularly indebted to in the Resources section at the end of this book. Some of the methods I'll be showing you are well-known in the force-free dog training community, while many have my own particular twist.

My work revolves around puppies, new rescue dogs, growly dogs - and, of course, dog owners. There are many people more gifted than I who can train animals to do astonishing things. My gift lies in being able to convey my knowledge to the dog's caregiver in a way which has them saying, "It's so obvious when you put it like that!"

Dogs are individuals and so are their owners, so sometimes creativity and imagination are needed to solve a problem. There isn't a one-size-fits-all approach to training - as you'll see when you look at the Troubleshooting sections following each lesson in the book.

Follow the steps that I outline for you. Don't skip or jump ahead. Work on each step till it's more or less right, then move on. There's no need to be a perfectionist here. You don't want to get stuck.

I suggest you read the whole book before you start so you yourself are clear what you need and what you are aiming for. Then re-read the lesson you're working on and go straight into your very short session. After this you can assess where you are and check the Troubleshooting for any difficulties that relate to you and your dog. Then you're ready for your next session the next day.

So stay with me, follow the directions, don't expect instant miracles, and we'll start changing your walks to comfortable, companionable outings. Most importantly, you will get the companion dog you wanted all along.

Chapter 1
Equipment that will help you…and equipment to avoid like the plague

Coco is choosing to trot along beside me with no pressure on his neck

I'm going to show you not only what equipment you need, but also what equipment you *don't need*, and - importantly! - what equipment to avoid at all costs.

First of all, let's take a quick diversion into anatomy. There is a myth that a dog's neck is somehow different from ours and can withstand the crushing effect of a collar cutting into the throat without any damage whatsoever. This is clearly nonsense. You only have to hear a dog choking as he heaves into his collar or see his eyeballs sticking out, his tongue going blue, and his face creased with the strain to know how wrong this myth is.

In fact, physiologically a dog's neck is *virtually identical to ours*. The trachea, thyroid gland, and oesophagus are all in much the same place. The nerves and blood supply to the brain are similar.

Now, imagine a constricting force on your own neck. What's going to be affected? Your eyes, your throat, your thyroid. lack of blood to the head, distress, fear, pain, and a feeling of being trapped and threatened. Some of these things are temporary, but some can have a permanent effect, and while the damage can be physical, mental damage will also be caused by this pain and aggravation, resulting in stress and anxiety.

Every time this happens, your dog is making a firm association that "walking on a lead means pain and bad things."

So if it's so bad, why on earth do dogs do it?

Dogs, as you'll hear me say repeatedly, are simple creatures. As I said before, they are doers, and they do what works. They aren't straining to pull you somewhere because they have a secret agenda or want to show you who's boss. They are pulling into their collar because they want to get somewhere and you usually follow them!

When they're very young, they don't have to pull that hard for the indulgent owner to stretch out an arm and follow. How often do you think they have to try this before it's a habit? Once? Twice? How often does a child need to see where the chocolate is kept to know which kitchen cupboard to head for? Once, I'd say!

When the dog gets a bit older, larger, and stronger, his owner becomes less forgiving, and he has to pull a lot harder. Sooner or later the pulling wears down the owner's resolve, and they follow their dog. This is why the lead responsiveness and parking exercises you'll find in the Key Lead Skills are so important to work on. You don't need to pull the lead or yank it. Just don't follow!

But my dog is big and strong!

Your dog doesn't need to be large to damage your shoulders with his pulling. A small and determined terrier can exert a lot of force on the lead. If you have a dog who already pulls like a train as soon as the lead is clipped on, then you'll need to dress her in something different while you train her to walk nicely on her collar.

Collars are very useful for attaching ID tags and for quickly holding onto in the heat of the moment, but they aren't essential dog gear. Your dog can wear a harness whenever you're out - provided it's the right kind - or, of course, your dog can wear both.

Collars

Some dogs don't like their collar being touched. They've been hauled about on the collar or dragged somewhere they didn't want to go. I'm horrified when I see people literally dragging a fearful and reluctant puppy along behind them on his bum!

Keep this in mind if you have a rescue dog: rescue dogs may have had a boatload of unpleasant experiences and can be very hand-shy. You might see this as they duck and dive when a hand reaches out toward them. They may also try to grab the hand with their teeth or just freeze in position.

You need to start by changing your dog's view of a collar-hold to a thing of beauty, not fear. Here's an exercise you can do repeatedly, perhaps when you're relaxing after dinner. Keep it brief and fun.

The Collar Hold

1. Reach towards your dog's neck, withdraw your hand again, and then with your other hand give her a tasty treat. Repeat till she's happy with your hand coming towards her neck. She shouldn't flinch or try to grab your hand.
2. Touch your dog's collar, take hand away, and give her a treat. Repeat.
3. Slip your finger into the collar, *remove your hand*, and give her a treat. Repeat.
4. Put your hand through the collar so that the back of your hand is against your dog's neck. You are not gripping the collar. Give her a treat. Remove your hand. Repeat.
5. Walk with your dog beside you. Have your hand through her collar but don't use it to pull her - treat.
6. Repeat each step till your dog is comfortable with it - this may take minutes, days, or even weeks. In time your dog should see your hand approaching and offer her collar to you, then stay still while you slip your hand in, with the back of your hand resting against her neck.

Do buy or use:

The collar should be comfortable to wear, easy to put on and take off, and quick-drying if your dog enjoys swimming. It can be soft webbing, soft leather, or woven fabric - this last is especially useful for puppies as you slot the fabric onto the buckle wherever you want.

I prefer snap collars to buckle collars because you can adjust the size millimetre by millimetre instead of being stuck with pre-punched holes.

Martingale collars made of soft webbing are particularly useful for sighthounds, bull breeds, and any other dog whose neck is larger than its head. These slip over the head and can fit very loosely on the dog's neck - but once the lead is attached they are impossible to back out of. Adjust this collar carefully, fitting it so it doesn't tighten and constrict the neck. It's not meant to be a choke collar.

Any piece of equipment is only as strong as its weakest part - so check clips, fabric, stitching, the soldering on rings, and so on, before you buy. Don't go cheap.

Don't buy or use:

Avoid collars that work by hurting. This includes prong collars, slip collars, chain collars, half-chain collars, choke collars, and *anything* that uses a battery. If you have any of these in your armoury, please destroy them - don't pass them on for some other hapless dog. (An exception to the no-battery rule is the "buzz" collar for deaf dogs, which vibrates like your mobile phone and serves to catch their attention.)

Remember your dog's neck is just as delicate and sensitive as your own neck. Or your child's neck. Thankfully more and more countries are making these instruments of torture illegal.

Harness

Do buy or use:

The harness I personally favour is the *Wiggles Wags and Whiskers Freedom Harness*, listed in the Resources section at the end of this book along with a link to a demo video. You are not so much looking for something to prevent pulling, rather you want a harness designed to promote balance. You are looking for a harness which attaches to a double connection lead in two places - in front and on the back. You want a harness that does not impede shoulder movement, does not chafe or rub, and has the effect of balancing your dog.

The object of using a harness is to prevent the dog pulling into a collar and damaging herself. It can also make Loose Lead Walking a doddle, as the dog has to support herself on her own four feet - without using you as a fifth leg - but it has to be the right sort of harness! Look for one which has the same effect as the one shown in the video.

Don't buy or use:

Some harnesses are designed to encourage the animal to pull, like a horse in harness pulling a cart or a husky pulling a sled. They aren't unpleasant: they're just not the right tool for this job. Others are sold to prevent pulling. Sadly many of these work by hurting the dog - by cutting under the armpits or by tightening and staying tight. Your dog will soon be pulling through the pain just as with her collar.

Head Halters

These require some skill to use humanely, but are useful if your dog continually has her nose on the ground. If the dog lurches to the end of the lead and is stopped abruptly, the head collar could cause her head to twist. It's essential that the lead stays loose when she's wearing it, and you don't flick or jerk it. Gentle pressure to turn the head is what you need but it can take a bit of practice. The best way is to slide your hand right down to where the lead clips onto the head collar and move the dog's head from there. This will ensure you don't yank the lead.

Do buy or use:

Only use a "fixed" head halter (example, *Gentle Leader*). Some figure-of-eight head collars will relax as soon as the pulling stops and are safe to use.

Don't buy or use:

A slip halter, or slip collar-halter combination - all of which tighten and stay tight if the dog pulls.

Leads

Leads are much more important than you may think!

Perhaps you see your lead as a controlling device, a way to move or restrain your dog. What we are working on here is to give the control to the dog, so she can exercise *self-control*. We want her to have the choice to keep the lead loose. Revolutionary, I know! So think of the lead as a connection between you and your dog - as well as insurance that she won't end up under a bus.

In order to give your dog the freedom to walk easily beside you, the lead must be long enough. Six feet is a good length. If the lead is too short, as soon as she moves an inch she's on a tight lead! Most leads you find in pet shops are ridiculously short - three feet or so.

When you're holding the lead, break that habit of winding it five times around your hand then continually flicking and jerking it! Many people have no idea that they're doing this, but every flick or jab is another nail in the coffin of your relationship with your dog.

The lead should be held loosely in your sensitive hand. If you need to prevent yourself jabbing the lead, tuck your thumb into your belt or pocket to keep it still.

If you have to keep your dog on-lead all the time, you'll also do well with a 15-foot long line for when you're in an open space or field. Don't use this line when you're on the road! This length is comfortable to handle and gives your dog the freedom to mooch about and snuffle without danger of her running off. It's important to "flake the line" in your hand - to have it in loose bows or figures-of-eight instead of coils that can tighten and trap a finger. It's the same system sailors use for the rope attached to a fishing net - so that it can pay out freely without getting caught, or catching a leg in a loop and taking a sailor overboard with it.

Do buy or use:

You want a soft fabric or leather lead, at least six feet in length. The lead needs to be light and comfortable to hold in your hands with no sharp edge to the webbing. A multipoint lead where you can adjust the length of the lead is very useful.

A long line of around 15 feet is easiest to handle. There are longer ones, but they're more useful to leave trailing for recall work.

Don't buy or use:

What you do *not* want are extendable leads, bungee leads, anything made with chain, cheap sharp-edged webbing, or a lead less than four feet in length.

Why no extendable lead? These contraptions actually teach the dog to pull! Every time she pulls, she gets more lead. There are also several safety issues around them. I know of cases where the mechanism has broken and the puppy has run into the road and been run over. I also know of cases where people have sustained serious burns to their legs or hands - and in one case, their neck - by the cord racing through the mechanism with a heavy speeding dog on the end. And then there are the dogs who panic when the clumpy plastic handle is dropped and bounces along the road behind them as they flee into danger.

The worst thing is that there is no sensitivity or sense of connection with a plastic handle. It's a lazy and ineffective option.

Devices used by the Inquisition

By now I hardly need tell you to ditch anything that uses fear or intimidation to get results. So into the bin goes anything you throw at your dog, rattle at her, squirt at her, or anything which uses a battery. *

Please destroy these things - don't pass them to another dog owner!

This is a companion you want to enjoy walks with, not an enemy who has to be kept under control with threats and abuse!

When I've explained how leads and collars work to the owners of a dog I'm working with, I'm always pleased when they tell me they've put all the inappropriate items in the bin - so that no-one in the family can use them again on their family pet.

This specifically excludes the excellent Manners Minder aka Treat-and-Train, which delivers a treat remotely to your dog to mark good behaviours at a distance from you; also "buzz" vibrating collars for deaf dogs.

What's a clicker and do I have to use one?

A clicker is a little gadget you hold in your hand and click to mark the very second your dog is doing something you like. The click is always followed by a treat. It's an excellent way of teaching - especially teaching complex behaviours.

But no, you don't need to use one. If you want to work on more complex behaviours with a clicker at some stage, do a bit of reading up on it first to make sure that you do it right. For now, your hands are going to be full enough with lead, treats, and perhaps gloves if it's cold, so don't worry about it.

You should still mark something you like, though! Marking gives the dog the precise information of what it was that earned her a reward and what she needs to do in order to get rewarded again.

Just as effective at indicating your pleasure at what your dog is doing is to say, "YES!" enthusiastically. Say it quickly, the instant she does the thing you like.

Treats

Here we reach one of the most important pieces of equipment!

Your dog needs to know just what you like and just what does not cut it. Every time she does something you like, you can mark it ("YES!") and give her a treat.

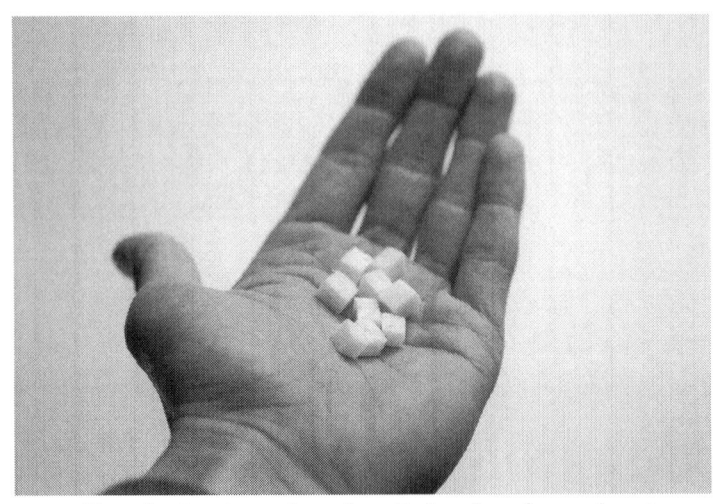

Your dog is going to love these little cubes of tasty cheese!

Good treats

- Cheese
- Sausage
- Ham
- Chicken
- Frankfurter
- Salami
- Homemade sardine, tuna, or ham cookies
- Freeze-dried 100% meat treats
- Dehydrated liver, heart, lung, etc.

…real food in other words. Ideally, they slip down quickly so your dog wants more. Cut them into small, pea-size treats.

OK treats

- High-quality grain-free commercial treats

Fairly rubbish treats

- Your dog's usual kibble (She gets it anyway. Why should she have to work for it?)
- Cat biscuits
- Dog biscuits
- Stuff of unrecognisable composition sold as pet treats
- Anything you wouldn't put in your own mouth

Do you work more enthusiastically for £60 an hour or for 50p an hour? Quite so. Your dog is the same. Be sure the treats you're offering are worth working for!

Troubleshooting

Why do I have to keep giving my dog treats? Shouldn't he do what he's told anyway?

I only give my dogs a treat when they've done something I like. I aim to get through a lot of treats every day! Treats are not a moral issue. They are a means to an end. The end is your dog walking willingly beside you on a loose lead. If employing a few bits of cheese means that my walks are enjoyable and my shoulder will not need rehab, then that seems a good deal to me.

But isn't all this extra food bad for him?

You're using high-quality food for treats. It's not like giving chocolate to a child. You have to feed your dog anyway, so you may as well get some mileage from it. If your dog tends to be overweight, simply remove an equivalent amount of food from his dinner.

Can I carry on using my present equipment?

Nope, not if it isn't on the approved list above! Make life easy for yourself and get the right tools for the job.

I use a short lead, because she always pulls to the end of it anyway.

Not any more, she won't. Once you've perfected the exercises in Chapter 2 she'll know that it's her job to keep the lead loose. A 6 or 8-foot lead will give her that opportunity, and you won't be following her! We'll be getting down to the nitty-gritty in the next chapter. You have to build the foundations first, and giving your dog the freedom to choose is an essential part of that.

What's wrong with extendable leads?

They're dangerous, insensitive, difficult to control, and unreliable. They actually teach your dog to pull! There is no connection between you if you're holding a lump of plastic attached to a thin cord. What do you think a top showjumper would say if you told him he had to hold a plastic handle instead of feel his horse's reins between his fingers? You'll be learning more lead skills in this book which will give you amazing control with the lightest of touches.

In this section we have discovered:

- It's vital to get the right equipment to make your walks enjoyable
- It's critical to stop using anything that causes stress, anxiety, or pain
- To teach your dog to love having her collar held
- "I'm paid to keep my lead loose - now I get it!"

Chapter 2
Change your mindset first

Coco strides out proudly, knowing exactly where he's meant to be

This is not a case of "them and us". We're talking about going for a companionable walk with your doggy best friend.

First of all, imagine going for a walk with your human best friend. You'd walk together and probably fall into step. You may hold hands or link arms. You'd chat and laugh. You'd point things out to each other as you pass them. You may interrupt your conversation to say, "Look at this flower," and you'll both wander over to examine it. Your friend may say, "What's in that shop window over there?" and you both - arm in arm - go to study it.

This is a pleasant walk. This is what you want to aspire to with your dog. So the first thing to do is change your mindset from having an adversarial outing to a companionable one.

This includes allowing your dog the opportunity to be a dog.

Unless you've got a train to catch, your walk can have many sniff-points. It's a chance for you both to unwind and explore your surroundings. Your dog will point out to you lots of things you never noticed before! You don't have to go 100 yards this way, turn left, 300 yards that way, turn right… etc. You can just go where the fancy takes you. You'll get your exercise just the same, don't worry!

Now I hear you cry: "But that's not what it's like! My arm is being ripped out of its socket! He has no interest in me!" So let's start from the beginning.

Holding the lead

The lead is not a gadget for restraining your dog, nor a device for hauling you along! The lead is there to keep your dog from running under a bus, possibly to help with her self-control when she wants to greet someone, and, *most importantly*, it's a connection between the two of you. Messages go up and down this lead. Keeping it tight with a vice-like grip will prevent any communication.

Go back to the walk with your friend. Do you grip his hand so tight it hurts? Do you yank him over to look at your flower? Does he turn on his heel without a word and haul you over to the shop window?

No! You're enjoying a walk together.

The same is true of you and your dog, and changing your view of the lead is the first thing to do. It may surprise - nay, astonish! - you to learn that if you keep the lead loose, your dog will keep it loose too.

It takes two to tango, as the saying goes, and it takes two to have a tight lead.

One of us has to stop pulling, and as we're the ones with the bigger brains, it needs to be us. Sadly, this pulling has often started in puppyhood and is now an entrenched habit. When people have their cute new little puppy, they tend to let it pull them all over the place. They think it is kind.

It is not kind.

It's teaching the puppy to damage her throat and neck as you saw in Chapter 1, and to ignore the person on the other end of the lead. So they have their pup on a lead. The puppy pulls towards something. Their arm stretches out. The puppy pulls harder. With outstretched arm they follow the puppy.

What has this puppy just learnt? "If I pull, they'll follow. And if I pull harder, they'll follow faster."

For some reason that escapes me, people find this appealing. Once the pup has grown a few months and can get some traction and force, not so much.

You never have to pull your dog's lead again!

Here's an exercise for you to change this entirely. You can do it in the kitchen first, then graduate to the garden before trying it on the road.

Key Lead Skill No.1
Holding the Lead

1. Have your dog on a longish lead (at least 2 metres)
2. Stand still and let the dog pull to the end of the lead, wherever she wants to go
3. Keep your hand close to your hip. Tuck your thumb into your belt if necessary

4. *Wait.* Wait till the lead slackens the tiniest bit. It doesn't matter why. You may think you'll need to wait forever, but it's usually only 20 seconds or so at most

5. As soon as you feel the lead relax - for any reason at all - call your dog and reward her with a tasty treat at your knee

6. Repeat till she understands that it's up to her to keep the lead loose

This exercise is simplicity itself. It tells your dog that you are no longer the one that's pulling. Your hands are soft. It's her choice if she pulls. Given a little time, she'll choose not to pull at all.

If your dog is in the habit of lurching to the end of the lead as soon as it's on, you may have to repeat this exercise frequently. In most cases we need repeat it only long enough to get the new system of lead-holding *into our own heads*. Once we've got it, our dog will get it.

Remember, dogs are doers, not not-doers. So your dog is learning to keep the lead loose, rather than not to pull on it. See the difference?

What you accept is what you get

Every time you put the lead on your dog, you need to remember to keep your hand close to you and *wait* for her to slacken the lead. If you are in the habit of putting on the lead and letting your dog pull you to the door, then that is what will happen.

What you reward is what you get.

There are few better rewards for most dogs then heading out through that door! Your dog needs to learn that - no matter what happened in the past - things have now changed, which means pulling on the lead will get her nowhere. Dogs aren't dumb. They do what works.

From now on you will never move until the lead is slack.

NEVER!

If you find your arm floating out, recapture it and tuck it into your belt! If it keeps happening, put one of your children on "arm-watch." They'll love having the chance of pointing out your mistake to you!

Time to keep still

Once your dog has learnt to keep that lead loose, and stay more or less near you, you can start on the next Key Lead Skill. It's incredibly useful and keeps your dog calmly under control without any effort from either of you.

If you want to stop and chat to someone, make a purchase in a shop, or wait at a bus stop, you can put the handbrake on and park your dog. This is a great way to immobilise your dog without any vestige of force or anger. This is how you do it:

Key Lead Skill No.2
Parking

1. The first thing is to hold your dog's collar. Rather than waving your arm about trying to catch the collar on a leaping dog, simply run your hand down the lead till you reach the collar, and slip a finger under it.

2. While holding the collar (gently!), allow the lead to fall to the floor and stand on it right beside your dog's front paw. Hang on to the handle all the while.

3. Now you can let go of the collar, straighten up, and keep holding on to that handle. A 6-foot lead is ideal for this.

4. Ignore your dog. No more interaction between you.

Your dog can take any position she likes. She's simply unable to pull or jump up. Your hands are free to delve into your purse or drink a coffee. Your visitor is safe from being jumped on. Your dog will find that as nothing more is happening, sitting or lying down is a good option.

When you get fluent and quick at parking, you'll have a way to anchor your dog easily. Be sure to hold the collar before trying to stand on the lead or you'll find yourself doing the can-can as your dog flies forward while you try to get your foot on a waving lead!

Before we move on, let's take a look at what's buzzing around in your head.

Troubleshooting

This doesn't work. My dog still pulls like a train, choking and spluttering.

Hang on! We're only at the foundation stage. You're building a different response in your dog's mind: it takes time. Keep working on these two exercises several times a day till your dog becomes as light as a feather on the end of the lead. For saner walks meanwhile, have a look at Chapter 1, where we discussed the pros and cons of various gadgets sold to aid Loose Lead Walking. There'll be something there to help you improve your walks humanely.

Do I have to give my dog treats?

Oh yes! We give treats to the dog to show her that we like what she just did. This means she will do it again. Why would you want to stop this sequence? The treats need to be good ones! Not manky old cat biscuits and fluff from the depths of your pocket, but what a friend of mine terms "crack cocaine cookies" - small chunks of beefburger, garlic sausage, ham, cheese, dried liver - irresistible morsels that are worth working for.

It's ok till we see another dog or person then all hell lets loose.

Chapter 3 will come to the rescue, but don't skip ahead! It's important to establish the foundation skills. We're just beginning. Don't expect miracles -

just yet! It may have taken your dog years to get to this level of lead-pulling expertise, so it won't change overnight.

I'm waiting for her to stop pulling, but she just keeps on. How long should I wait?

Wait till she stops. I know you think you'll both be standing there till Christmas - but really, it's more like a few seconds. If you're very close to something - for example, if you are nose to nose with another dog - then this is too hard and you'll need to back off. Methods for doing this without hauling your dog backwards in the upcoming chapters.

If I stop every time she pulls, we'll take forever to get anywhere.

Too true, but you're not trying to get anywhere yet. You're teaching your dog that it's up to her to keep the lead loose. This is an essential first step, so keep working on it at every opportunity.

He's ok with me, but the children nearly get pulled over.

If you have a dog who pulls hard or who is unpredictable (that's most of them), it's not appropriate for a child to be walking him. Depending on the size of the dog and the maturity of the child, you may be able to supervise walks with your child holding the lead when he hits early teenage years. Safety is key. I taught my children never to put their hand through the handle of the lead and to let go of the lead if the dog pulled. I'd rather have a run-over dog than a run-over dog and a run-over child. But I never let them get into such a situation.

I shout at her to stop pulling, but she ignores me.

She probably thinks you're egging her on! Here's the thing: dogs do *not* understand negative concepts. They are doers. They need to be doing something. *They can't not do anything.* So we are going to reframe the whole adventure into a "do this" format, instead of a "don't do that" one. Stay with me - it'll become clear!

We've hardly begun and you have learnt

- To honour your dog so you can enjoy walking together with her
- To hold the lead in such a way that you *never* have to pull the lead ever again
- To keep your dog stationary without shouting, intimidation, pushing, or pulling
- "Wow! My throat's not hurting any more!"

Chapter 3
If she's not out front, where should she be?

This is the Reward Spot. Coco knows just where to be to earn his reward

We've established that dogs can't *not do something*. They have to *do something*.

We're going to start by showing your dog where we'd like her to be when we are moving. She has to know where to be in order to be there!

Choose which side you'd like your dog to walk and stick to that side for the time being. It doesn't matter which side. It simply makes everything much easier for *you* to learn while you get your mechanics right. She can walk either side in a few weeks once you've got it.

It's you who has to do some learning here. Just like driving a car, if you grate the gears and stamp on the pedals your car is not going to perform well. To get a smooth "drive" with your dog, you're going to need to learn these Key Lead Skills carefully. Your dog will say, "Oh, *that's* what she wants!" and it will all become a breeze.

Let's say you want to walk your dog on your left side - I'll give you directions for that. If you prefer the dog on your right side, just reverse all the lefts and rights below! So you'll be holding your lead and your treats in your right hand. Your left hand will stay empty (no lead, no treat).

To show her where she should be when she's on lead, we'll teach her the Reward Spot. Whenever she's there, she'll get a treat. It's the place she has to be to get us to move forward - that spot is by your left leg, with her head at your trouser seam.

Don't get tangled up with the details - just remember that this is a game you're playing with your dog: you're challenging her to catch you up at your left leg no matter what you may do to escape!

Lesson 1: Teaching your dog to find the Reward Spot

1. Start this in a quiet place - my dogs all learn this in the kitchen! To begin with, a one-minute session is good. Always keep these sessions very, very short.

2. Stand with your dog roughly on your left. Your lead will be held loosely in your right hand with a big loop reaching almost to the floor in a J-shape. Have 10-15 tasty treats in your cupped right hand. Turn a bit so your dog has a good chance of reaching your left side first, wherever she's coming from.

3. As your dog comes towards you, say, "YES" *Then* take a treat with your left hand, touch your hand to your left trouser seam at dog nose height - this is your Reward Spot - and feed the treat to her as she arrives.

4. Take one step away to the right and wait for her to look at you or move towards you - "YES!" - down comes another treat to your trouser seam and into her mouth!

5. To begin with, she won't be that close to your leg, just paying attention. The gap between her and you will gradually close as she wants to get that treat.

6. Repeat this till she realises that getting close to your left leg produces a treat: take a single step away from her (sideways, backwards, or occasionally forwards). Keep this speedy, rhythmical, and fun. After a while you'll find it hard to get away from her! She's saying, "Ha! You can't catch me out!" and whooshing into your left leg.

7. At this stage it doesn't matter which way your dog is facing, and it doesn't matter if she jumps up or paws you. Just wait for her feet to hit the floor before you reach for the treat.

8. If she gets lost or confused, coming into the wrong side, or if she wraps the lead round you, just do a quick 180 degree turn to unravel her. Give her the greatest chance of success at hitting your left leg.

9. Make it as easy as possible for her to succeed. *We're teaching, not testing.* You may need to keep turning to ensure she hits the correct side and learns where that Reward Spot is. "Ooh, you clever girl!" you can say, as you turn so that she finds herself on your left side.

Watchpoints

- Don't hold the treat out to lure her to come to you: "Please, doggy. Please!" Don't beg her! Wait for her to work it out. *After you've said, "YES,"* you fetch a treat from your other hand, touch it to your leg, and feed. She may be slow to catch on at first, but once she knows you have food, she just has to figure out how to get it. You may need to keep both hands together to prevent one slipping down your leg before she's got there!

- Always touch the treat-hand to your leg. What we're teaching is technically a Nose Target - telling our dogs, "When your nose is close to my leg, you get a treat." Those of you who've read the first book in this series, *Calm Down! Step-by-step to a Calm, Relaxed, and Brilliant Family Dog*, will recognise the concept of targets - in that case, when getting your dog to land on her mat it was a paw target - now it's a nose target. When you call your family down to dinner, they don't wander off into the garage or to the front gate, they come to the table! That's where the food arrives. So touching the treat to your leg at dog-nose-height means that that's where she'll come to get it every time. If you make a mistake and feed straight to her mouth, she won't have this certainty about where exactly she should be. Six inches away? A foot away? A yard away? Make this crystal clear, and it will be much easier for your dog!

- A large dog will be very close to your side, with her Reward Spot at your hip. A small dog may stay a little further out from your leg to avoid being trodden on and to be able to see your face. Her Reward Spot will be much nearer the floor! If you have a problem bending this far, smear some pure peanut butter, liver pate, or squeezy cheese onto a wooden spoon and hold that down by your ankle for a quick lick each time you've said, "YES," then lift it up again.

- Be sure to keep the lead loosely in your right hand - the opposite side from the dog - and looping down in a nice J-shape that allows your dog freedom. Be careful not to flick or tighten the lead. The plan here is for your dog to stay by your left leg because she wants to be there. She's not there because you make her. It has to be her choice!

- Be sure to feed with your left hand - same side as your dog. If you feed with your right hand, you will be quite unable to touch your food hand to your left trouser seam - making the Reward Spot a fuzzy area - and you'll be drawing your dog round in front of you. You want her head level with your leg.

- Only take *one step* in any direction - we're not walking yet! We're just establishing the position to be in when the lead is on. Don't jump ahead!

- If you're finding this confusing, try without the dog. Really! Just like dancers have to get their steps right on their own before trying with a partner or a group, you can get the lead and treats into the correct hand, imagine what your dog is doing, then run through a few goes. This may help you get your mechanics down.

Dogs learn by rhythm and patterning. The more rhythmic and fluent (and quick!) you can make your session, the faster she'll learn.

Once you've got it, your dog will get it very quickly.

Your first tentative steps

You may need to take a week or more teaching your dog her Reward Spot. Have at least one - preferably two or three - one-minute sessions every day. Every time you put the kettle on is a good time for a session, or every time you've been to the bathroom. You can build a habit that makes it very easy to fit your training into your already busy day. You can encourage your dog to find the Reward Spot whenever you call her - just turn as she's arriving and touch the treat to your trouser seam. This is her new Best Place Ever!

Up to now, having her nose near the Reward Spot has been enough to earn a treat regardless of where the rest of her body is. Once she's hitting that spot every time, we need to let her find the Reward Spot in such a way that she ends up the right way round.

Here you go:

Lesson 2: Reward Spot on the Move

1. Do a few treats' worth of Reward Spot as usual, just moving *one step* away from your dog in any direction. Make sure she always stays on your left side - help her if necessary by turning your body. Don't test her by getting her the wrong side of you. Softly, softly …

2. Very fluently - *without any break in the rhythm you've built up* - drop a treat just behind your left foot. While your dog is scarfing this up, take one step forward (two steps for anything larger than a collie).

3. Your dog will look up, see you've moved, and rush to catch up with you as you look back over your left shoulder to admire her.

4. As she arrives at your leg - "YES!" - down comes another treat for her, touched to your trouser seam in the reward spot.

5. Instantly, in the same rhythm, place another treat behind your left foot.

Repeat steps 2 to 4, building a fast rhythm. Now your dog is diving for the treat, spinning round and landing next to your left leg - more or less the right way round!

Once you've established the Reward Spot, right on your leg, it's the same whether you are standing, walking, running, hopping, or calling your dog to you.

Instead of a complicated system of Loose Lead Walking, your dog only has to learn this one thing: always be at my person's left side with my nose near their leg. How easy is that? I will be showing you some more games, but basically it's all *Reward Spot on the Move*.

Troubleshooting

My dog doesn't stop at the Reward Spot - she flies ahead!

What enthusiasm! With a fast dog you need to be fast too and anticipate her. As she lifts her head from eating the treat, you say "YES!" By the time the word has come out of your mouth, she should be just passing your leg. She'll look up because you said, "Yes," and get her treat from her Reward Spot. Working in a small circle - with her on the outside - may help to slow her down. Don't worry if she's going past and then coming back to you, facing the wrong direction when she arrives. Practice makes perfect. She'll soon learn that the game goes faster if she stops on the way!

My dog is sniffing around after he's eaten his treat from the floor.

Be sure to use treats that don't crumble. Crumbly biscuit or flaky chicken will cause him to go into search mode every time he puts his nose down. This will teach him to hoover. Soft, slippery treats he can grab in one go then spin round are what you need.

She goes to get the treat, loses the plot, and wanders off.

You may need to ensure the floor is clear of toys and other distractions, but the key here is to establish a rhythm and get it going fast. She should be bouncing into position beside you. If she's distracted by a sound, make a kissy or clucky noise to get her focus back to you. A noise is better than using her name. On no account chide her - or it will no longer be a fun game.

You say to keep the lead loose, but I have to keep it short or she goes too far away.

Then she'll never learn to stay in place of her own volition. You have to give the dog a choice so she can make a good decision (which earns her food) or a poor decision (which earns her nothing at all). If you keep her in place with a short lead, she's limited in her choice, so she can't make a good one! Does that make sense? Persevere with a loopy lead and see how it begins to work when your dog has the freedom to make a mistake. It doesn't matter if at this stage she's bouncing back and forth. She'll settle as the game becomes clear to her.

Why only one step? I want to get moving!

Patience, Grasshopper! You'll be moving soon enough. Imagine you're learning the piano. You don't start with a Beethoven Concerto. You start with simple tunes, scales and exercises to build up your knowledge and ability. If you can get your dog flying into the Reward Spot every time after one step (two steps for larger dogs), you'll be ready for the next stage, but don't be in a hurry to push the supports away - we want a firm foundation so your building stays up!

We had the Reward Spot perfect, but once I take a step we lose the rhythm.

Do what you may have done for learning the Reward Spot and try without the dog. Once you get a rhythm handling the treats, placing one down, and being ready with the next at your leg, you may find your dog trots over and joins in!

He takes the treat from the floor, turns very slowly, and plods up to my leg - where he stops and sits. Is this right?

All dogs are different. Maybe you have a large heavy breed like a Mountain Dog, that do things more slowly than - say, a Working Cocker Spaniel, who do everything at 100 miles an hour. So if that's the fastest he ever goes when walking, then that's fine. If you're only taking two steps, he should arrive with you as soon as he's turned, so doesn't need to follow you - yet. Moving more than two steps will come later. If he wants to sit when he reaches your leg and you're stationary, that's also fine. Some people like to teach a sit every time they stop. This tends to come with practicing the Reward Spot on the Move. If your dog is very dozy and slow, have a quick, short game of chase or retrieve in the garden first to get him engaged with you and more lively. He needs to enjoy the session and not be bored silly!

In this section we have learnt

- How to give your dog a fixed spot where she should always be when on lead
- Showing her how to find that spot when you move
- That rhythm and patterning will establish the habit
- That it's a process of building the understanding - not launching onto the street and expecting your dog to know what you want
- "I like bouncing back and forth! I like being in this spot."

Chapter 4
Keeping those hands soft at all times

Soft hands on the long line, gently turning Meg away from a distraction

Keeping your hands soft on a floppy lead can be hard to do. You've spent ages holding the lead tight as if your life depended on it, restricting your dog's freedom.

Now we want the dog to have freedom - freedom to choose to stay beside us! - so making sure you keep your hands soft and the lead loose is going to go a long way towards this. If your dog sails off away from you, you need to be able to stop her without yanking her off her feet. You want her to slow down, turn, and choose to come back to you. The lead needs to stay fluid so nothing sudden happens.

I know you're thinking if you loosen the lead, she'll pull all the time - but that's the old thinking. You now know that giving your dog the freedom to choose and then rewarding the choice you want will have her making good decisions in no time. As she learns these new skills, things will be changing dramatically before your eyes.

So let's look at how you can slow your dog to a gentle halt without pulling.

You really never have to pull your dog's lead again!

Key Lead Skill No. 3
Slow Stop

1. Your dog is heading away from you, perhaps in pursuit of a good scent, or trying to reach someone.

2. If she walks on your left, you'll have the lead in your right hand. You are using a lead of at least 6 feet in length, aren't you?

3. As she moves away from you, loosely cup your left hand under the lead, letting the lead run through freely, *gradually* closing your grip so she can feel this squeezing action as the lead slows down.

4. This will slow her sufficiently to ease her into a stand.

5. Now relax your hands and lead - you may need to take a small step forward to let your hands relax and drop down - and admire your dog standing on a loose lead.

6. You can attract her back to the Reward Spot with your voice - treat, and carry on.

This should all be calm, mostly noiseless, and easy. It's like holding your friend's hand and gently slowing them down till they come back into step beside you. No need for "Oi!" "Stop!" "C'me here" or anything else other than saying, "Good Girl!" and giving her a welcoming smile when she reorients to you.

Try this first with another person instead of your dog to help you. Ask them to hold the clip of the lead in their hand, turn away from you and let the lead drape over their shoulder, with you holding the end behind them. As they walk away and you start to close your fingers on the lead, they should be fully aware of that sensation and respond to it. They'll be able to tell you very clearly if you're gently slowing them or jolting them to a stop! Your dog too will recognise this feeling on the lead as "Oh hallo, we're stopping now."

When you start, it may take a few attempts to get your dog to stay still and balanced when she stops so that you're able to relax the lead. After a while she'll know that this rubbing sensation on the lead is the precursor to a halt. The right sort of harness will help enormously to get her to balance on her own four feet instead of using you as a fifth leg. See Chapter 1, and the Resources section at the end of the book.

Troubleshooting

My dog stops alright, but as soon as I relax my hands, she surges forward again.

It's good that you've got the slow stop. Now you relax your hands just a little (an inch or so) to test whether she's standing balanced on her own feet. If she immediately starts to lean forward again, ease her to a stop again - maybe just using your fingers on the line - and test again. Sooner or later, she's going to realise that slow stop means stand still.

I can stop her pulling forward but she just stands looking ahead, so I give up and follow her.

You're halfway there! Once you've slow-stopped her and relaxed your hands you can now *wait*. Unless there is something super-attractive just in front of her, sooner or later, she'll look back at you to see if you've died. Now you are doing Key Lead Skill No.1 and can encourage her to your knee for a treat. If you walk her on the left, for instance, that treat can be delivered at her Reward Spot. Now you can go forward. Dogs are clever, but they are not (always) mind readers! Help her.

Sometimes she'll come back to my leg before we go forward again.

There's something you're not telling me here! "Sometimes" she does it perfectly suggests that sometimes she does not and you go forward anyway. This is going to confuse your dog: "Is today one of the days I can pull forward?" She needs to know that pulling on the lead will *never* get forward movement. Now she'll be much faster at coming back to her Reward Spot until she gives up on pulling forward altogether. Can you remember when your mother would say, "What's the magic word?" when you asked for something without a "please"? You soon learnt that saying, "Please," got you what you wanted without that annoying delay! This is a gradual process. It will come. Your task is to be utterly consistent: from now on, whenever your dog is on a lead you are training her!

I've been doing this stop-go stuff for days now, but she still wants to pull forward.

Keep going! This doesn't happen overnight. In a few weeks you'll be surprised how much things have changed. In a year you'll have forgotten she ever pulled at all. If you give up now, she'll carry on pulling happily forever. It takes time practicing it in the house or other distraction-free areas before you can get it to work on the road. And patience - a lot of patience.

You really, really, never have to pull your dog's lead again!

Where this can come unstuck is when your dog pulls away from you and resolutely stays pulling away. You are diligently following the instructions outlined in Chapter 2 for Key Lead Skill No.1 *"You never have to pull your dog's lead again!"* but your dog just stays there, leaning into the lead.

This is probably because she is distracted by something that is so close that she can't shift her mind away from it: another dog right in front of her? Some dropped food? A favourite person approaching?

If you don't like the look of the dog in front of her, the food looks dangerous, or there's a truck driving towards you - you need to be able to move her, fast.

If you try to drag her backwards out of the situation, you are pulling against all the strongest muscles of a dog - her back and haunches. Think of the strength a carthorse exerts to get a cart moving and think how hard it would be to pull against that power.

You need another lead skill so that she turns toward you of her own volition, *without you trying to haul her backwards!* Here it is:

Key Lead Skill No. 4 Lead Stroking

Meg responds to the stroking by turning back to me

1. Your dog is at the end of the lead and too close to the distraction to respond. Maybe you need to move her because of danger or for good manners.

2. Move yourself slightly to one side or the other so that you are in her peripheral vision. Bend towards her in a friendly and playful way. Dogs have 270-degree vision as opposed to our 180 degrees, so you don't have to move far.

3. While making clucky, cooing noises - don't bark her name - start stroking the lead gently.

4. Use a hand-over-hand action, as if you were pulling a rope in - but *you are not pulling*, just stroking! Your stroking action would be the same pressure you might use to stroke a baby's hand.

5. Watch her collar or harness to ensure that you are not tightening the lead and pulling.

6. As you stroke and make super-attractive noises, your dog will look round, see you, and start to turn towards you.

7. Engage her eyes with yours, happily congratulating her, and back away a few steps, still bending forwards.

8. As soon as she's disconnected from the distraction you can turn and carry on walking.

9. You can give her a treat as you trot away, telling her how good she is.

You *never* have to pull your dog's lead again.

Troubleshooting

I'm doing all this stroking but she's still pulling ahead. I have no choice but to pull her backwards.

Up your level of enthusiastic "coochy-coos" and the moment her head turns towards you, move backwards while she engages with you and gives you eye contact. Don't turn until you've got this connection. If she's still rivetted on what has distracted her, try walking sideways, perpendicular to her, to make it easier for her to join you before you back off.

This is great! She turns really quickly to join me, but as I jog away she's leaping up beside me.

As long as she's not grabbing your sleeve I'd be delighted with the jumping. It shows you've taught this really well as a game and she's keen to turn from her distraction to play with you. If she wants to grab, have a soft toy ready for her to sink her teeth into.

The very beginnings of your companionable walk

No, you're not heading off for a loose lead walk right now - but you're getting there …

First I want you to incorporate your new lead skills into your walks, just a little at a time. The more fluent you are, the easier this will be, and the more responsive your dog will become.

If your dog starts to surge, you can choose one of your new Key Lead Skills. You can wait for her to realise she needs to get back to you in order to move forward, you can start to slow down, bringing her to a slow-stop, or - if she's stuck - stroke the lead with kissy noises to draw her back into your world *without pulling!*

You can use your ordinary 6-foot lead for this, or if you're in a larger space you can use your 15-foot line - don't use a long line near a road. I'd recommend you walk your dog on a harness for now, too. The right sort will remove a lot of stress from both of you! See Chapter 1 and the Resources Section at the end of the book for guidance on the right harness to get.

Troubleshooting

My puppy doesn't pull - she just sits down and won't budge! I don't like dragging her along the pavement.

Please don't drag your puppy along! If she's having a sit-down strike, it could be because she's tired. Young puppies need only minutes walking on a hard surface. If she's not tired, it's most likely because she's anxious about what's ahead. That leaf she saw fluttering in the breeze could be a snake or other monster. The shape ahead she can't identify could be a bottomless pit! As for the motorbike parked at the side of the road - a Martian?! When she sits, just relax your lead and give her time to assess the danger. It's all new to her! After a while she'll look less worried and stop fixating on whatever it is, then you can make your attractive sounds, tickle the lead, and she'll come trotting along with you again. It's an important part of her Habituation and Socialisation process that she has time to study things that may worry her.

My dog wants to sniff the hedge all the way.

Try walking further out from intoxicating smells like the hedgerow. Stop and re-engage him. More techniques for getting his attention on you are in the next chapter, where we'll be taking this on the road!

My dog plods along so slowly behind me.

Breeds are different in their behaviour. My Whippet Cricket likes to walk just behind my feet. Rollo the Border Collie can't get anywhere fast enough! If your dog is a heavy or giant breed, speed may not be his watchword. As long as he's keeping up with you, a slow pace can be enjoyable. If he seems to be labouring, he is not old, and it's not very hot, there are two things to check: he may be overweight, or consider a vet check for nagging joint problems.

My dog is 8 years old and she's always surged out ahead of me. Is there any hope of changing this?

It's clearly a well-established habit, but *yes*, you can change this. Maybe she'll always like to be a bit ahead of you, but that's ok as long as she's not pulling! Follow this system and you can eliminate the pulling.

I've damaged my arm. It's really difficult to hold the lead and the treats.

You'd better use your good arm for the lead and treats for now. Slow things down a bit. If your dog is not huge and doesn't lunge violently, a very good method is to attach the lead to your belt or tie it round your hips, so that you're hands-free. Round the hips is better than round the waist, which can stress your back - your hips are pretty stable. Try this in a safe place to see how it goes. You may find that in addition to resting your arm you are cutting out all the unconscious flicks and jabs you were doing with the lead, and your dog will respond much better!

In this Chapter, we've learnt

- To use two Key Lead Skills to change your dog walking experience for ever
- To exercise patience and gentleness when walking with your dog
- "I'm free to sniff and explore without my neck hurting!"

Chapter 5
Get moving!

Rollo enjoys a pleasant walk with me, his lead loose

- Your dog knows the Reward Spot
- She can find it when you're moving
- You've got the four Key Lead Skills

Now we're going to get moving!

1 2 3 Treat!

If you want, you can just get moving using the Reward Spot, rewarding your dog whenever she's there at your leg and looking at you. For some people this works really well, but most prefer this next stage which really cements all the stages together into a fluent walk. For this, you are going to be counting out loud with each step you take - "1, 2, 3, Treat!" then you stop.

To begin with your dog will have no clue what you're doing, but if you are rhythmic in your stepping and counting, very soon she'll get the message that treats are on offer every fourth step and she will make sure she's beside you when you say "Treat". You are teaching her to check in with you every few steps - what you would expect from a companion on a walk.

Lesson 3: Checking in

1. Get yourself ready with your dog by your side, lead and treats in the opposite hand. Treat her in the Reward Spot so she knows what game you're playing.
2. Start counting *out loud* rhythmically with each step as you walk forward: "1, 2, 3, Treat!"
3. Stand still.
4. If, when you say, "Treat," your dog is there at your leg, you touch the treat to your trouser seam and feed her. If she's wandered off, wait for her to turn back to you, then treat.
5. Immediately step out again, counting. It really is that simple! Don't overcomplicate it.

Troubleshooting

My dog is wandering off before we even start.

Be sure to treat him in the Reward Spot so he knows something is happening. Move quickly into your counting so he hasn't lost interest before you begin.

We start off well, but she keeps going behind me and switching sides.

Keep an eye on her - look down over your shoulder so she can see you and not feel the disconnect that leads to her doing her own thing. This isn't a test! Make it as easy as possible for her to succeed by staying with you - chat to her.

Now she's watching me all the time!

And that's a problem? You've done well to get her to enjoy this game and stay beside you where she can comfortably watch you. Over time you'll both relax and walk more naturally. She doesn't have to watch you like an Obedience Champion, as long as she checks in with you every few steps. Just let it flow for now.

I have to wait ages for her to come back to me. She zips to the end of the lead as soon as I say, "One."

Go back to working the Reward Spot on the Move in Chapter 3, so she remembers she's meant to be by your leg. Once that's going fluently again, just move into this game and start counting. She should be right with you!

Every time I turn she manages to get on the wrong side of me.

I suspect what's happening is that you are walking forward evenly then suddenly, perhaps because you've reached the wall of your room, you spin round. She is caught by surprise, but quickly tries to stay with you - inevitably on the wrong side of you! So instead of walking in straight lines with sharp turns, try to find a space where you can walk in a large circle or oval with your dog on the outside. Maybe your driveway. If you have one of those splendid kitchens with an island, you have a ready-made, purpose-built, Loose Lead Walking training ground!

When do I add my word "Heel!"? She doesn't seem to understand it.

There are two questions here. No dog understands any words until they're taught what they mean. The way to teach a word is to pair the word with the action you want. So you say, "sit" as your dog's bum is going towards the ground, for instance. You need to describe what she's doing while she's doing it - that way she'll make the connection. Having said that, let's look at the other question - about using a vocal cue. I haven't suggested you use a word for loose lead walking at all. The reason? It's a default behaviour which needs no words. The way you stand and hold the lead tells your dog what to do. Dogs pay much more attention to our body language than to what we say. Whenever your dog has the lead attached your motion produces the desired action of keeping her by your leg. You don't need to tell her! I do say, "Let's go!" to my dogs when I'm starting to move - perhaps when we've waited for the traffic to clear to cross the road. This is just to give them some warning that I'm moving. They put themselves in the right place.

She's great up till she gets the treat, then her mind and nose are elsewhere.

This is not uncommon if you lose the rhythm. She thinks she's done the right thing by staying with you till you treated her (and she's right!), but while you pause to think of what to do next she reckons it's over and goes off sniffing. So as soon as you treat, say, "One," and step off smartly. This is where the rhythm is so important. No gaps.

Remember: dogs learn by rhythm and patterning!

You don't need to march like a soldier or take giant steps! Walk naturally, but smartly and rhythmically - just as you do when you're walking with a purpose, as opposed to ambling or shuffling along.

Be careful not to overdo it

As with the other techniques, do just a little at a time to begin with. Don't bore your dog!

You'll find you quickly get fluent at 1, 2, 3, Treat, and you should soon find yourself walking along smartly, your attentive dog at your side! You'll need to adjust your stride and pace slightly to accommodate your dog's size and pace.

A very small dog may need you to take smaller steps to keep with you. A large, rangy dog will require you to stride out manfully.

Find what works for your dog first. It can be hard for a large dog to walk very slowly - she's always having to dot-and-carry-one to stay with you, possibly going sideways at the same time. So stride out and find a pace which works for her. Once you have this going smoothly and fluently, you can start to ease the pace slightly so your dog stays at the same gait while making smaller steps. A trotting dog always works better than a walking dog.

Eventually you'll reach a perfect compromise between what's comfortable for you and easy for her.

Let's take this on the road

As with the previously-learned techniques, start to incorporate 1, 2, 3, Treat into your walks just a little at a time. Choose a point in the walk when your dog is not too excited and there's little distraction around. Feed in the Reward Spot and start counting.

Don't worry that people will think you're batty! They will actually be impressed by your stylish teamwork. You won't be marching along counting for the rest of your days, but you don't want to jettison the counting too soon. It's a prop and a connection to remind your dog to keep checking in with you.

When you're going for that companionable walk, hand-in-hand with a friend, you look about then check back in with them, perhaps to talk. That's what your dog and you will be doing on your walks - enjoying the walk together and checking in with each other.

As you get proficient, you can turn your 1, 2, 3, Treat exercise into normal walking, gradually cutting down the treats as you go - and stopping the counting out loud! Don't rush ahead but consolidate each layer of training before you move on.

More advanced stuff

So the next thing you do is to stop the stopping. You count, - "1, 2, 3, Treat" - touch your leg and feed while moving. Continue this rhythm: "1, 2, 3, Treat," touch your leg, feed while moving, "1, 2, 3, Treat," touch…

Now you are flowing along together, walking rhythmically, smiling happily at each other whenever your dog checks in with you. You're ready to cut back on some of the treats - by counting every other step.

You can count two steps to each number instead of one step. So where you were going: 1, (step) 2, (step) 3, (step) Treat (stop), you are now going: 1, (step, step) 2, (step, step) 3, (step, step) Treat (step, step) … and so on. Keep a rhythm going.

When this is flowing you can venture out to: 1, (step, step, step) 2, (step, step, step), etc.

If at any time you "lose" your dog, go straight back to the original 1, 2, 3, Treat till she's back with you, then start stretching it out again.

Really advanced stuff

One of the ways to ensure your dog always stays with you is to practice walking at different paces. You've established a suitable pace which stretches out your dog into a trot while allowing you to walk at a comfortable speed. Now you can practice slowing down gradually to a very slow pace, then speeding up again - maybe moving into a slow jog till going back to your normal pace.

The purpose of this is to enable your dog to stay with you, whatever your speed. This will make her more attentive and make the walk more interesting. It can also turn into a great game of "You can't make me go wrong!"

And here's a helpful system to get past attractive smells. Those of you who have already read the second book in this series, *Leave it! How to teach*

Amazing Impulse Control to your Brilliant Family Dog, will recognise this concept. If you haven't read it yet, that joy is still to come!

Lesson 4: Moving past distractions

1. When you're walking along the road and you come to a grassy area which is going to be rivettingly exciting for your dog, just carry on walking past it while your dog says, "I really want to sniff here!"

2. After a few paces, turn back and pass it again. Maybe your dog still strains to get to the grass - keep walking!

3. Now turn again and go past it again. Continue this process.

4. At some stage your dog will realise she's not getting on the grass and will walk nicely with you - BINGO!

5. The moment she decides to stop pulling to get to the grass is the moment you reward her by giving her permission to sniff it. Tell her, "Go sniff!" and give her a minute on the grass.

She's learning that pulling towards something she wants is not going to work, but that if she looks longingly at the grass while keeping with you - maybe, just maybe, she'll get there.

That's not to say you are going to reward her by sending her to sniff at every opportunity! On a walk there are going to be some sniff-points where you can have a break and let her have a mooch around. Dogs don't get to sniff every tree and lamp-post as you walk, but there's no harm in occasionally stopping to admire the "view."

Congratulations on working through this far! You have now found the Holy Grail of dog ownership: *Having your dog walk beside you on a loose lead!*

This is what your dog has now learnt:

- Where she should be in relation to you when on lead
- That she can look around as long as she frequently checks back with you
- Nobody is going to pull her lead, so it's up to her to keep it loose

And you have both learnt:

- Walking with your dog is a pleasurable activity, not a battleground
- It takes two to tango. If you pull, she'll pull
- It takes time to adjust to each other's stride
- "Walks are more fun when I'm not pulling!"

Chapter 6
Complications?

Lacy barks at someone in a funny hat

You are on your way to mastering a system to teach your dog how to walk nicely with you on a loose lead. If your dog is even-tempered and friendly, you're now all set for a lifetime of happy walking - but there are some dogs who have additional issues. These are dogs who have fears and anxieties about the world we live in - maybe they're afraid of people, other dogs, children, joggers, cyclists, traffic, plastic bags, loud noises… You name it, there are dogs who are afraid of it. Known as "Reactive" or "Fearful" dogs, there are an awful lot of them about.

You may not guess from their reaction that they are actually afraid! They are so desperate to keep the thing they fear away from them that they bark ferociously, lunge forward on the end of the lead, and put on an Oscar-winning performance of intimidation and noise that distresses their owner and frightens everybody else.

Maybe you've seen these dogs and wondered why their owners would have such a nasty dog and why they can't control them? Maybe you have one yourself and you know your dog is a devoted, delightful family pet who's brilliant with the children. She's much loved by the whole family - who are baffled about why she does this. And you're at a loss to know how to help her.

If this is you, be assured that there is a way to work with your lovely dog to help her gain confidence so she's no longer at the mercy of her fears popping up in front of her everywhere. It's outside the scope of this book, but there's lots of help for you at

www.brilliantfamilydog.com/growly

Here, you'll find an extensive free course to get you started, all - just like this book and the rest of this Essential Skills series - entirely force-free.

No.1 Tip: Give your dog as much distance as she needs to be able to manage without getting upset

This may be 10 yards, 30 yards, 100 yards, or whatever she needs.

"My dog's friendly!"

If your dog is a paragon of social virtue, a friendly sausage who loves everyone, spare a thought for those who are not so fortunate. It's easy to look down your nose and condemn. Before I knew first-hand what it's like to have a fearful dog I was supercilious myself, but with experience comes understanding and compassion.

The best thing you can do when you see someone struggling with their dog - who in turn appears about to burst into a frenzy of barking - is to give a friendly smile, *lead up your dog*, and head away.

Calling out, "My dog's friendly!" as your loose dog rampages towards the other dog is no help whatever! If this is someone you see regularly, your friendly, non-boisterous dog may indeed be helpful one day to demonstrate to their anxious dog that not all dogs are dangerous, but you need to give the fearful dog as much distance as she needs to be able to cope - only very, *very* gradually getting nearer. This may take the reactive dog months without any help.

With help we're talking about a transformation within weeks.

Direct the struggling owner to www. brilliantfamilydog.com/growly so they can get that help.

The owner of a Growly Dog should expect a gradual improvement rather than an overnight fix. In a month or three they'll be looking back and saying, "Wow! We couldn't have done that calmly before."

No owner or dog has to suffer this level of anxiety and misery - there is light at the end of this tunnel!

In this Chapter you've learnt:

- Not all dogs are created equal
- Fear is a very strong motivator
- "Aggressive" dogs are not usually aggressive
- "Please look after me!"

Conclusion
A new life ahead of us

By the time you've worked through this book, you'll have new systems in place. You and your companion dog will be on the same page! You'll both understand what the other wants. You are now able to look forward to companionable walks without stress and without the danger of being pulled over in the mud, shouting, getting cross, and asking yourself, "Whose idea was it to get a dog?"

You'll be building gradually, keeping in mind that you're going through a complete re-training phase. If you're lucky enough to be starting this with your brand-new puppy you'll never have to re-train! You'll have it right from the start.

While this is going to be the new habit, give your dog time to remember each time where she's meant to be, and keep those rewards flowing freely whenever she does something you like!

Spin-offs

Now your dog walks calmly beside you on a loose lead - instead of head down, scrabbling along the pavement, pulling your arm out - a new world will open up to you. You can take your dog everywhere with you! You'll know that she will behave well on the lead regardless of the distractions. You can walk her with your hands full of shopping bags. You can walk her while you're holding the children's hands and know she'll take care to accommodate them and their erratic speed.

You can enjoy coffee at a café without her lurching about on the lead and putting her paws on the counter. Likewise a drink in a pub will be a pleasant experience once she knows it's her job to keep the lead slack. See *Calm Down! Step-by-step to a Calm, Relaxed, and Brilliant Family Dog* to learn how to get complete peace and quiet while you relax! When you nip out to post a letter your dog can bring you the lead and you'll set off together - rather than you thinking, "Oh no this is too much trouble! I'll go on my own."

You'll be able to enjoy all the things you planned to do when you first got your dog. You'll get fitter, meet more people, shed those pounds, and enjoy the great outdoors. All because you and your dog have learnt a few new skills with the lead.

So your dog will have much more freedom, a more interesting and stimulating life - with visits to beauty spots, nature trails, beaches, the local shops. Most importantly, she will spend much more time with the person who is the most special thing in the world to her:

You.

Top up the learning

Once this is all in place, it will be a simple thing to ensure your dog stays in her Reward Spot. Your hands will be soft on the lead. If she starts to follow her nose away from you, you can simply pause and slow-stop her gently. She'll remember where she should be and pop back beside you. It will take a while for this to become automatic - for both of you. Up till then you are in teaching mode.

Resources

If you've got any specific queries, you can email me direct at beverley@brilliantfamilydog.com This will come straight to my personal inbox and I'll answer you - usually within 48 hours. Try me!

Meanwhile, for more free training, go to www.brilliantfamilydog.com and get a series of instructional emails on common day-to-day problems, like jumping up, chewing, barking, and so on.

> Thank you so very much for all your excellent advice. *Lisa*

> I just wanted to drop you a quick line to say how great your emails are. There are always a few lines in each one which are corkers! Fluffy pup / piranha fish, well yes, that I know now! It's also so nice to know that this is normal. *Laura and Waffle*

> Just to let you know that Molly is progressing really well thanks to your tips. *Anne and Molly*

> I really appreciate your emails: they are very helpful! *Norma and Tonto*

And www.brilliantfamilydog.com/growly is for those of you with anxious and fearful dogs.

And if you've got any specific queries, you can email me direct at beverley@brilliantfamilydog.com This will come straight to my personal inbox and I'll answer you - usually within 48 hours. Try me!

Harness

www.goodfordogs.co.uk/products for UK and Europe (see video)

I supply these harnesses to the British Isles and Europe. If you get one through me I will benefit financially but it won't cost you any more. Watch the video. If you can find another harness that has the same effect, go for it!

http://2houndswholesale.com/Where-to-Buy.html for the rest of the world

http://dogmantics.com/is-it-harmful-to-attach-a-leash-to-your-dogs-neck-2

You can get a hands-free lead which fixes round the hips if you want to do jogging, skijoring, and canicross with your dog.

For Challenging Dogs

www.brilliantfamilydog.com/growly
www.goodfordogs.co.uk/aggressive-dogs.html
www.fearfuldogs.com
www.controlunleashed.net

Essential Skills for a Brilliant Family Dog

Book 4

Here Boy!

Step-by-step to a Stunning Recall
from your Brilliant Family Dog

Beverley Courtney

Introduction

This dog is showing his owner a clean pair of heels

"Ditzy! Ditzy!! DITZY!!! C'me 'ere Ditzy. Ditzy NO!"

Ditzy didn't hear much of this. She'd heard it all before, so she carried on her merry way. "Di-i-i-itzy!"

First, she snatched a biscuit from a toddler's hand. "Ditzy come here this instant!"

Then she romped off and jumped up at an old lady who tottered backwards before being caught by a passer-by. "DITZY!"

Delight of delights - she found some fox-poo and joyfully rolled in it. "Dit-ZEE!"

Einstein said that doing the same thing over and over again and expecting different results is a sign of madness - this owner sure was mad by now!

It took several more minutes of mayhem before Ditzy had run herself out. She knew from all that shouting that her owner was cross so she slunk back slowly. She endured the lead being snapped on roughly and getting a noisy telling-off all the while.

How likely is it that Ditzy will come next time she's called?

If her owner had only realised that dogs don't come with a recall installed, that it was up to her to teach her dog to come when called, that it would be fun and only take a few minutes every day! Then the toddler would still have his biscuit, the old lady would not now be having palpitations, the owner wouldn't be in the shower trying to get the stink off her dog, and the walk would have been enjoyable instead of the embarrassing mess it became.

In other words, if she'd had this book, things would have been very different! You'll find that teaching your dog an ace, high-speed, instant, recall is not only easy, but FUN - for both of you. On top of that, you'll develop a new bond with your dog which doesn't depend on you barking orders and her (not) obeying - rather, you'll develop a companionship where both of you are reliable and consistent, and you'll enjoy your walks together.

I've been teaching force-free methods to dog-owners and puppy-owners for years, and it's a joy to watch the dog-owners change from sergeant-majors who are trying to confine and control their dog, to easy-going and relaxed - secure in the knowledge that their dog will spin on a sixpence and come barrelling back to them when they call. They and their dog have so much freedom!

So how would you like to have a bombproof recall with your dog?

If you follow the guidance in this book that's just what you'll have! This book is the fourth in a series of **Essential Skills for your Brilliant Family Dog**. It stands alone - but combined with the other three (you can find them in the Resources section) will give you a huge insight into how to get the results you want from your dog - without force, fear, or friction.

- I'll guide you through the process step-by-step
- I'll troubleshoot your training sessions so you make them as efficient as possible in the short time you have available in your busy day
- I'll show you a recall from your dog's point of view, what works, what doesn't, and why
- What progress you can expect and when
- Best of all - I'll show you how to have fun with your dog again! Isn't that why you got a dog in the first place?

If you can spend just a few minutes every day working through this program as I unfold it to you, I promise that your dog's recall will transform beyond all recognition. You'll have a dog who can come away from people, playing dogs, running children, food - even rabbits, in time!

This means you'll have a dog who enjoys far greater freedom to run and frolic.

Is this what you want for your dog? They say that the best time to plant a tree is thirty years ago, and the second-best time is today. Are you going to take the first step towards making a huge change - or carry on shouting furiously at your misbehaving dog? Are you going to get stuck into this straightforward and enjoyable program - or carry on having frustrating walks? Are you going to dazzle other dogwalkers with your dog's scintillating sharp recall - or are you going to carry on apologising to crying children and frightened old ladies, and dreading the moment when you hear screeeech-BANG as your dog races across a road?

It was having to learn the techniques to make a Brilliant Family Dog with my own busy household of multiple dogs, cats, sheep, goats, hens, and children that set me on the road to helping others do the same. I learnt early on that forcing someone to do something only resulted in grudging compliance at best; whereas getting them to participate and enjoy the process turned them into eager and fast learners. This applied equally to the dogs, the goats - and the children! The sheep and the cats not so much.

My qualifications range from the understanding of learning theory to specialist work for fearful, anxious, and growly dogs. Acquiring an anxious, growly dog of my own ensured that I learnt and understood the process of assimilating the dog into our world in a way which builds her confidence.

There are some superb teachers and advocates of force-free dog training, and you'll find those I am particularly indebted to in the Resources section at the end of this book. Some of the methods I'll be showing you are well-known in the force-free dog training community, while many have my own particular twist.

My work revolves around puppies, new rescue dogs, growly dogs - and, of course, dog owners. There are many people more gifted than I who can train animals to do astonishing things. My gift lies in being able to convey my knowledge to the dog's caregiver in a way which has them saying, "It's so obvious when you put it like that!"

Dogs are individuals and so are their owners, so sometimes creativity and imagination are needed to solve a problem. There isn't a one-size-fits-all approach to training - as you'll see when you look at the Troubleshooting sections following each lesson in the book.

And no - it's not difficult to teach. Follow the steps that I'm going to outline for you. Don't skip or jump ahead. Work on each step till it's more or less right then move on. (No need to be a perfectionist here - you don't want to get stuck.)

I suggest you read the whole book before you start so you are clear about what you need and what you are aiming for. Then re-read the lesson you're working on and go straight into your very short session. After this you can assess where you are and check the Troubleshooting for any difficulties that relate to you and your dog. Then you're ready for your next session the next day.

Straight away this book will show you just what makes a recall work and how you can get your dog onside from the start. You'll learn the force-free secrets the pro trainers use to get an instant response from their dog - without any shouting, cajoling, or mean tricks - and you'll learn the one thing that will completely change your dog's attitude to you!

Get started right now - turn your dog into a star and enjoy the process as well as the results!

Chapter 1
What you need to have and know to get success

Archi is comfy in his well-designed harness

To help you while you're working on everything you'll learn in the following chapters, I want to show you first how you can make your life a lot easier - and your dog so much more biddable. If you've read the other three books in this **Essential Skills Series** you'll know that I start each book with the tools you need for the job. Don't be tempted to skip ahead! This chapter is particularly tailored for recall work.

Treats: what and why?

Don't get hung up on the whys and wherefores of using treats in dog training. How would you feel if your boss said to you, "I know you enjoy working for me. I know you do it just to please me, so don't expect any pay this Friday!"

It's not a moral issue. It's not like giving chocolate to a child. You have to feed your dog anyway, so you may as well get some mileage out of the food. We are paying our dog for work done with good food, and - just like us - your dog will respond better to better rewards.

While I always have some dried liver or even high-quality kibble in my pocket - so that there is never a time when my dogs may not be rewarded - when I'm working with them on something new or important I bring out the heavy artillery. This means I use treats that my dog will sell her soul for, not dry kibble and pocket fluff. You can get some first-class commercial treats if you hunt very carefully, but the best treats tend to be soft, slippery, flavoursome, smelly, and home-prepared - real food in other words.

I frequently use cheese, sausage, frankfurter, pepperoni, and suchlike. You can make sardine, tuna, or liver cookies. Dehydrated meat, especially liver, is also popular, provided it's small and goes down quickly, so your dog is ready for the next reward without having to spend half an hour chewing the last one and forgetting what she earned it for.

If you're concerned about weight gain for your dog, then take out an amount equivalent to what she's earned during the day from her food bowl. If you stick to the suggestions above and give good quality food as treats you will be improving her diet too!

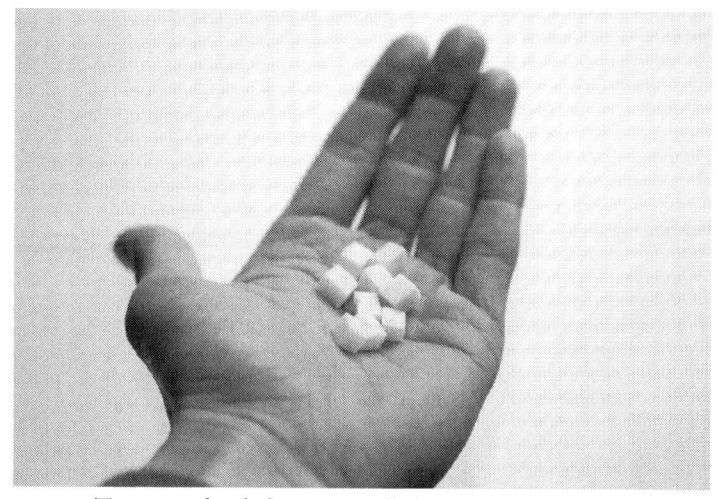

Treats need only be very small, but must be very tasty!

Good treats

- Cheese
- Sausage
- Ham
- Chicken
- Frankfurter
- Salami
- Homemade sardine, tuna, or ham cookies
- Freeze-dried 100% meat treats
- Dehydrated liver, heart, lung, etc.

…real food in other words. Ideally, they slip down quickly so your dog wants more. Cut them into small, pea-size treats.

OK treats

- High-quality grain-free commercial treats

Fairly rubbish treats

- Your dog's usual kibble - She gets it anyway. Why should she have to work for it?
- Cat biscuits
- Dog biscuits
- Stuff of unrecognisable composition sold as pet treats
- Anything you wouldn't put in your own mouth

Generally speaking, the harder the task for the dog, the better the reward needs to be. So if you're playing a training game in the kitchen you can make do with fairly ordinary treats. Out in the big bad world, with dogs and children flying around shrieking, squirrels running up trees, wind in the leaves - when you're teaching Ditzy the skills needed to come back from the child's biscuit, the old lady and the others she's previously terrorised - then you need the best stuff!

Remember this is all about choice. Your dog is choosing to do what you want instead of following her own inclination.

Control the rewards and you control the dog

Think about this: to control the rewards you have to know what your dog finds rewarding, and here I'm including not only what we can offer her but also what she finds for herself.

Here are some thoughts on what your dog may find rewarding:

- Rolling in a cowpat
- Rolling for joy
- Sniffing, tracking, air-scenting
- Running wildly
- Jumping, leaping
- Barking, singing

- Playing, tugging, tossing, catching
- Playing with other dogs - chasing, grabbing, wrestling
- Catching balls, flies, treats
- Stalking birds, dogs, toys
- Chasing balls, squirrels, dogs, rabbits, cats, scent
- Greeting dogs, people, children, family members
- Fetching the lead
- Access to the garden
- Access to the car
- Access to your bed
- Access to the sofa
- Digging, burying
- Nesting
- Toys
- Chewing

You will surely be able to add a few peculiar to your own dog! You can see from this brief list that some of these rewards will be suitable for a training session, some can be used as a big release reward, and some are not at all suitable. I think rolling in a cowpat probably comes into that category - unless your dog's due a bath anyway! And if your dog is a confirmed rabbit-killer, you wouldn't want to use the "chasing rabbits" one. Otherwise you can use all of them. Keep in mind that some of these are hardwired instinctive drives. Where possible it's good to allow your dog to practice them in a safe environment, rather than trying to squash them. Attempting to suppress these behaviours is not going to work!

Serious note: If your dog is stalking and chasing lights, reflections, torch beams, leaves, or shadows, this is an Obsessive Compulsive Disorder which will get worse - much worse, to the point where your dog may become totally disabled. You should get professional help from a qualified force-free behaviourist as soon as possible. Never use it as a reward!

Here are some examples of how you can reward your dog based on her hardwired instinctive drives:

- You may call your dog, and as she comes thundering in you turn and race away. This is a *Chase and Running Reward.*
- You may throw her toy at her as she gallops in. This is a *Jump and Catch Reward.*
- You may throw her toy behind you, race her for it then play tug with her. This is a *Chase and Tug Reward.*
- You may dance, shout, and encourage your dog to join in. This is a *Barking Reward*!

As you can see, all those rewards encourage great excitement and involvement from your dog. What better way to make a recall the most exciting thing ever?

Remember too that you need to teach your dog her recall when she's already excited, not just when she's a bit bored at home. Think about it: you're going to need her recall most when she's excited, totally distracted, and zoned in on one of her chief rewards, so that's the state of mind in which you need to practice.

You may have a session of three or four recalls in a rabbity area, then release your dog to go and hunt rabbits as a massive reward. Here's where your dog may surprise you: she may prefer to continue interacting with you and forget about the bunnies. Really!

The lesson to take away from this?

Your dog's greatest distractions are your dog's greatest rewards!

What the stylish well-behaved dog is wearing

There is not a lot of equipment you need for this, but what you do have should be of high quality and secure.

Collar

Do buy or use:

The collar should be secure though not bulky. A snap collar which is adjustable millimetre by millimetre is best - especially for fast-growing puppies - rather than a buckle collar which has fixed widths between holes. A collar is only as strong as its weakest part, so check stitching, soldering on rings, and the strength of the plastic clasp. Choose a soft-edged material that won't chafe your dog's neck. Collars should be as loose as possible while not being able to be pulled over the dog's ears - you don't want her backing out of it on a road.

Don't buy or use:

Never use anything with chains, spikes, or electronics of any kind - with the single exception of vibrating collars for deaf dogs. If you want to use any of these instruments of torture, increasingly being banned by law in many countries, you're reading the wrong book.

Harness

Do buy or use:

For attaching a long line for recalls in an area where you are worried about safety, any four-clip harness will work. The harness I personally favour is the *Wiggles Wags and Whiskers Freedom Harness*, listed in the Resources section at the end of this book along with a link to a demo video. You are not so much looking for something to prevent pulling, rather you want a harness designed to promote balance. You are looking for a harness which attaches to a double connection lead in two places - in front and on the back. You want a harness that does not impede shoulder movement, does not chafe or rub, and has the effect of balancing your dog. Look for one which has the same effect as the one shown in the video.

Don't buy or use:

Some harnesses are designed to encourage the animal to pull, like a horse in harness pulling a cart or a husky pulling a sled. They aren't unpleasant: they're just not the right tool for this job. Others are sold to prevent pulling. Sadly many of these work by hurting the dog - by cutting under the armpits or by tightening and staying tight. Not for us.

Lead

Do buy or use:

Go for a comfortable, light lead of at least 6 feet in length. It can be good quality soft webbing or pliable leather. Some people favour soft, narrow, rope leads, or plaited leather. For puppies and small dogs, you can use a puppy house line of 8 feet. You can always leave the lead attached and trailing so it's easy to catch up your dog if necessary - though not in woodland or deep cover. It may give you more confidence to let her off in the first place. If calm lead walking skills have so far eluded you and your dog, head for the third book in this series of Essential Skills, *Let's Go! Enjoy Companionable Walks with your Brilliant Family Dog.*

Don't buy or use:

Anything made with chain, spikes, thin cord, cheap leather, cheap sharp-edged webbing, anything heavy enough for a carthorse, or shorter than 6 feet.

Tag line

This is a sawn-off lead of about 8 inches in length - short enough that your dog won't trip over it. Again it's an easy way to catch her if you need to. You may well have a lead that your puppy chewed that will do nicely.

Long Line

These come in varying lengths. For ease of handling in an off-road area, 15 feet is a good length, but if you're leaving it trailing for recall purposes, 30 feet works well. Any longer and you will be doing macramé with trees, dogs, and passers-by. Connect it to the back clip on a harness, not her collar. It should be light and not absorbent - or your dog will be dragging a ton of weight after her on a rainy day!

Don't buy or use:

Extendable leads in any form. They prevent a connection between you and your dog because of the plastic handle; they are dangerous; they teach dogs to pull; and there is little control.

Now you have an understanding of rewards and how to use them, as well as what equipment you may like to use, let's get on with your training!

In this Chapter you've learnt:

- The importance of the right equipment
- How some equipment will make things worse - much worse
- Rewards are not just food - let your dog show you what she finds rewarding
- "When do I get the frankfurter?"

Chapter 2
What is a recall?

Rollo is happy to be running full speed towards me, on one call

You need to know first of all just what you expect when you call your dog. You need to visualise the perfect recall - and that's what you'll be aiming for.

For me, the definition of a Recall is:

When I call my dog, she turns instantly and races back to me at high speed. When she arrives with me she stops and stays with me.

Picture this: your dog is mooching about in the hedgerow and you call her name. What's the very first thing you want her to do? If you said, "come back," you're missing a lot of subtle steps that can make or break your recall right at the start!

When I call my dog's name, I want her to turn and look at me. This may be very quickly followed by her barrelling back to me at speed, but the very first thing she did was acknowledge the call by looking at me. This is the first thing we'll be working on; getting that head-snap turn as soon as you call.

Like the sound of that? Good!

First let's have a look at some other important points.

Your brand new puppy

People often mistake their new puppy's infant clinginess for a recall. They think they don't have to train anything because their puppy already keeps close to them and comes when they call.

This will change! As your pup grows and gains confidence you will have to do battle daily with all the things she finds more exciting and stimulating than you. This will include many of the things on our list of instinctive drives, which your young dog will find irresistible. If you can start teaching the components of a mighty recall as soon as your puppy comes through the door at a few weeks old, you'll have it installed. You will be ready for when she hits adolescence around six months old and tests every boundary she sees, just like our teenagers do.

Call just once

This is one of the toughest things for owners to grasp! It works like magic once you've got it. Your dog needs to know she has but one opportunity to come and get a thumping good reward from you. The more you call, the less she will listen - just like Ditzy, whose name meant nothing to her. If you are broadcasting noise like a radio station why should she bother to come? She knows just where you are!

Calling repeatedly can also be described as nagging. Back to those teenagers again, who are expert at tuning out calls and requests - and accusing their parents of nagging them! We all know the response nagging gets in people. "Grumpy non-compliance" would sum it up. Don't do this to your dog too!

I'll show you how to get the response you want from your dog on one call. It's going to be up to you to provide the duct tape to apply to your mouth to prevent you from calling again and again.

Call Once - then Zip it!

Name versus sound

Dogs don't have a verbal language system like we do. You know how a toddler may say, "I eated it," when they're still learning the language? They've grasped the principle of the past tense but their vocabulary hasn't yet caught up.

Dogs don't have this ability to manipulate verbal language. They hear sounds, and those sounds represent things. When you say, "Sit," just as your dog is sitting, you are labelling that action as SIT. She'll recognise the sound and knows what action goes with it.

She'll also associate good or bad outcomes with that word. If every time you say, "sit," your dog gets a treat as soon as she sits, then she's going to like and respond to that word "sit." Supposing every time you say, "Sit," you abuse her and shout at her, it's not going to take long before the word "sit" has her running off to cower in a corner instead of joyfully and smartly sitting, anticipating a reward. Trainers call this a "poisoned cue". The word "sit" has come to mean very bad things for this dog.

The wrong association can happen without us realising it. You may have asked your dog to sit before an intrusive treatment - nail clipping for instance. "Sit" now means, "I'm going to do something to you that you don't like." Or, of course a rescue dog who's been mistreated in the past is going to have a lot of bad associations with a lot of common cues. You'll need to reteach her with a completely different word and only good outcomes.

So you can see from this how important it is to pair your dog's name only with good things! We all get annoyed or frustrated with others at times, whether it's our fault or theirs. If you are annoyed or frustrated with your dog, it's vital that you do not say her name! Her name is precious and should always get her heart racing and bring a smile to her mind and her face.

Here's a way to make sure she knows her name is wonderful and it's always worth responding to!

ACTION STEP Making your dog's name wonderful

1. For the next 5 days, whenever you notice your dog, say her name cheerfully - once.

2. As soon as she races to you with tail wagging - or just flickers an eyelid - reward her joyfully with a surprise - attention, fun, game, toy, or a treat.

3. Every third or fourth time she bounces to you, slip your hand softly in her collar, so she can feel the back of your hand against her neck. Don't grip hard. Then release it as you give her reward.

4. Repeat endlessly, all day long.

Speed, joy, and enthusiasm

When you call your dog, you are giving her an opportunity to race towards you and have a game. It should not signal the end of fun and freedom. When she comes back to you, she gets treats, love, fuss, and entertainment, then - more often than not - *you let her go again.*

Speed, joy, and enthusiasm - exactly what we want in a lightning-fast recall - must be built in from the start. Do whatever it takes to keep your dog lighthearted and eager to engage with you. If you need to sing and dance, then by all means do that. This will help you build a happy and enthusiastic recall - not a mopey, reluctant, slow-motion dawdle back to you.

While you don't want your dog to hit you at such speed that you are sent flying, I'd prefer that to a morose plod any day.

Follow through

When you call your dog (once!), she is going to end up at your feet. Period.

So make sure you only call her when you've got a high chance of her coming back. And if she doesn't? Don't think, "Ah well, I'll wait till she's less busy and try again." Go right up to her and call once from a yard away. She's almost certain to come then, and if not you can simply put your hand gently in her collar and call her. You're not pulling her by the collar, you are simply limiting her choices so she's more likely to choose to come to you. There's no need for crossness. She's learning.

Puppy vs. mature dog vs. new rescue dog

Your dog will respond differently according to her stage of development. I sometimes hear new puppy-owners proudly saying their dog's recall is perfect. *She's only 9 weeks old!* She's a baby - of course she wants to keep near you! Just wait till adolescence hits and your pup is adventurous and hormone-driven. You'll need a solid recall to cope with that. So use the time when your puppy responds quickly to you to build this in as a default behaviour.

I was chatting with a lady who had two dogs of about 6 and 7 years old. One of them was being particularly naughty. She said, "I can't understand why he's like this. He went to puppy classes …"

If only sending your child to kindergarten for six hours were all that was needed to educate him - it would save us a fortune in college fees!

I like Zig Ziglar's answer to this: "People often say that motivation doesn't last. Well, neither does bathing, that's why we recommend it daily."

Training your dog is an ongoing commitment which you "top up" every day.

Again like some teenagers, older dogs may have an established pattern of "selective deafness" - doing what they like when they like! Your new rescue dog will have all sorts of baggage and is unlikely to have had much friendly training. You will be building your new dog's confidence and trust at the same time as teaching her new skills. The system you are about to start on will work for these dogs just as well, but you have a bit of history to work against.

Pavlov (not the creamy meringue dessert, but the scientist)

A word about the way dogs learn:

You may have heard of Pavlov's Dogs. Pavlov was a Russian scientist who did a lot of pioneering work on the digestive system. As was common in those days, animals were used in the laboratory for testing. Pavlov used dogs. They were rigged up with a device that measured their salivation in the tests.

Pavlov noticed unexpected salivation occurring before the tests had begun. To begin with the dogs would salivate when they heard their food being prepared. Then they started salivating when the technician arrived in the building.

So Pavlov tried something new. He tried a number of sounds, including a bell. He rang the bell as the dogs were about to be fed. Sure enough - after some repetitions, they linked the sound of the bell with the anticipation of their food and pretty soon they would salivate at the sound of the bell without any food being present.

Pavlov had identified what came to be known as Classical Conditioning - the knee-jerk reaction that people have when they connect two hitherto unrelated occurrences. To us a doorbell represents a visitor and produces excitement and activity, but it's just a bell!

We can make good use of this principle to generate our astounding instant recall response! You can see now why I want you to pair your dog's name with only good things.

Dogs do what works

Dogs are simple souls. They do what works. If a certain action of theirs results in a reward - food, fun, entertainment - they'll repeat it. It's up to us to make sure that what we want them to do always results in what they perceive as a reward. It's really that simple!

It has further been proven that the predictability of that reward is key to getting consistent results. In the Marshmallow Test (detailed in the second book in this series of Essential Skills, *Leave it! How to Teach Amazing Impulse Control to your Brilliant Family Dog*) it was shown that if the tester appeared unreliable, the subjects would not comply with the testing procedure. They'd "cheat". In other words they wouldn't play ball.

If your dog finds that producing the action you want does not lead to reliable rewards, then she'll bail and not bother with this game any more. How long would you keep turning up to work on Monday morning if you only occasionally got paid on Friday? As a dog-owner, this doesn't mean your pockets have to be crammed with sausages for your dog for ever more, but it does mean that you must in some way reward your dog every single time she does what you want. We'll talk more about this later.

9 Rules for the Perfect Recall

Here's a list you can print and commit to memory for when you're out "in the field".

1. When your dog comes back to you - no matter what she's been doing or how long it took, it's the best thing she's ever done, even if you

need to count to 10! *The day you tell her off for returning is the day your recall will start to crumble.*

2. Always reward the recall - first-class food, toy, game, activity, enthusiasm.

3. Only call your dog when you have a 90% chance of her coming. Otherwise you are teaching her to ignore you. Close the distance and wait for the right moment.

4. Call in an exciting voice. Your voice isn't exciting? Then why should your puppy come?

5. Start indoors, then increase difficulty in small increments - different room, corridor, garden, enclosed field. Each time you move to a new area, go back to a very short distance recall.

6. When each stage is perfect, start adding distractions.

7. Nine times out of ten, call your dog, reward her - then *let her go* again.

8. When you're approaching a known run-off place, get your dog's attention beforehand. Engage her in an exciting game till you've passed the danger zone.

9. Do lots of mini-recalls in the house - whenever you notice your dog take the opportunity to reinforce her coming to you and responding to her name.

Both you and your dog should be having fun!

In this Chapter you've learnt:

- What makes dogs tick
- A little bit of science (I snuck it in there …)
- To say your dog's name only once, then zip it!
- What you may expect
- "I like this new way of thinking! I'll do anything for a sausage."

Chapter 3
Now the fun starts!

Ged the Bernese pup enjoys a game with his owner

It has to be fun. Dogs are all about fun. Make it fun and you have a willing partner. Make it "because I say so" and you will get grudging compliance, sometimes. They really aren't with us for very long - why would you want to be hard on them?

To keep up the fun, we're going to start learning our lightning-fast recall with a game. If you remember, the very first thing we're looking for is a fast head-turn.

Remember Pavlov and his Classical Conditioning from Chapter 2? He established the dogs' responses by repetition. Dogs learn by repetition and patterning just like we do. Those six puppy classes won't cut it! You interact with your dog daily - make sure your interactions are building something you want to see again and again.

As Pavlov's dogs' drooling was an unconscious response to the bell, your dog's head-turn is going to be an unconscious response to her name - a knee-jerk reaction. Just like an Olympic athlete in training, you'll be building muscle memory.

You'll be using a marker word ("Yes!") at the exact moment your dog does the thing you want her to repeat. She'll quickly learn that "Yes!" means she's done something right, earning her a reward. Then she'll start to try to get you to say, "Yes!" At that point, the training becomes totally interactive.

You can, of course, use any word you like, but "Yes!" lends itself to fast utterance. For me, it's more "Yiss!" than a sing-songy "Ye-e-e-e-s." If you choose "Good," you may find yourself saying "Gooo-oooo-oood!" which is way too long and has missed the moment entirely! You may use a clicker if you like - either way, the skill is in matching your sound precisely with the action you want your dog to repeat.

Learning to pay attention

Get yourself a handful of succulent and delicious treats, your dog, some good humour, three spare minutes, and a little floor space indoors. Be animated, quick, and enticing. Get your brain in gear and be absolutely ready to catch her first response! If you want your dog to focus on you, you must be able to focus on her - and focus on the outcome you're aiming for.

Lesson 1: The Focus Game

1. Stand and place a treat on the floor to the right of your foot. Your dog will eat it and possibly sniff about for more. Finding none, she'll look towards you to see if any more treats are coming.

2. Say "YES!" enthusiastically the second she turns to you and place another treat - quickly and with a flourish - to your left.

3. As your dog looks up from eating it, say "YES!" and place another treat to your right, and so on, getting into a fast rhythmic dance.

Once your dog knows the game you'll be able to throw the treat to right or left without having to bend over and place it. It's not a game of "Hunt the Treat," so be sure your dog sees where you drop it so she can grab it instantly and turn. A bowling action is better than a toss as your piece of cheese will land who knows where if you toss it.

It may take several short sessions before your dog is keen to run back and forth in front of you like a pendulum. This may take days - don't worry about a timetable. She's learning to focus on you, turning quickly to look at you after grabbing her treat. Repeat the Focus Game till it becomes totally automatic and slick for both of you - and always ends up with smiles from you and that zany expression on your dog's face.

Lesson 2: The Name Game

Now we can move forward to the Name Game. Here, we will establish that her name means a fast head-turn.

1. Start with the Focus Game, and once you have a rhythm, add your dog's name just as she's diving for the treat. She just has time to grab it and turn.

2. Say "YES!" exactly as her head turns. You are marking the muscle movement in the neck.

3. Repeat now till your dog is spinning round, ears flapping, just after you've said her name, and turning with joy and enthusiasm!

4. Stop while you're ahead! About ten treats or a minute or so is enough.

Watchpoint

Be sure you say your dog's name just as she's about to grab the treat then *follow* with "Yes!" for the head-turn, *then* toss the treat. The sequence is

> (toss treat)
> Name
> Yes!
> Treat
> Name
> Yes!
> Treat …

Develop a rhythm and make sure these are separate events. Don't let all the steps happen at once or confusion will reign!

Troubleshooting

My dog is moving quite slowly.

Unless you have a St. Bernard or another giant breed, who naturally move their great bulk more slowly - like an ocean liner turning - then you want to aim for speed from the get-go. Be more enthusiastic! Move quickly! Inject some urgency into the game! How fast does your dog move when she sees a rabbit or squirrel to chase? That's the speed you want!

He's turning back to me, but he's staring at the food in my hands!

Good observation. This is a natural response and is quite acceptable to begin with, but you will want your dog to start looking at your face. Make sure that your hands do not move until after you've said "Yes!" If the treat is being waved about or you're holding up your hand like the Statue of Liberty, that is what your dog will focus on. Hold your hands together until after you've spoken. If your dog is still fixated on your hands, put your hands behind your back. Once they're out of sight your dog will only have your face to look at: "Yes!" Treat!

My dog's not that interested in the treats and goes sniffing for ages after she's got one.

What treats are you using? Check out the list in Chapter 1. You need treats your dog will sell her soul for. Be sure they're not crumbly as that encourages hoovering.

She's doing it, but she's not that fast.

A common mistake is to say the words at the wrong time. You only have two words to say! Be sure that you're saying your dog's name at the *exact moment she's about to grab the treat*, not after she's picked it up. Your "Yes!" is to mark the head-turn, so say it just as her head begins to turn. By the time the word is out of your mouth it'll coincide with her muscle movement. She may not be going fast because she's unsure of what she should be doing. Oh, and call her name as if she's at the end of a field. If you say it quietly because she's right next to you, she won't be learning the sound you'll use when you're out and about.

I run out of floor space when I move.

Aha! You shouldn't be moving at all. You need only stand still. It's your dog who's doing the moving!

I show her the treat each time, but she's not very fast.

Don't do that! Your treat is a reward for your dog spinning back to you, not an enticement to work. The first treat you put down is just to get her away from you. If she's already distracted you could try skipping that one and moving straight into calling her name once. You do not want to teach your dog to see the colour of your money before she'll do anything for you. Showing her the treat, waving it about in the air, putting it towards her nose, is called "Luring" and will seriously limit how far you can go with your dog. There is a huge difference between rewarding and luring. Please don't disappear down that luring rabbit hole! Keep your hands to yourself when you're playing this game. If necessary, cup your hands together until the moment you place/bowl the treat. Stand upright and just use your voice to get your result.

The treats bounce and roll under the furniture!

Glad to hear you have an enthusiastic game going! Use soft treats (see Chapter 1) and don't throw them so vigorously. You can place them either side of your feet to begin with. You only need to bowl them further away as your dog gets into a speedy rhythm.

I'm not sure she's hearing me - she's just grabbing treats.

It's essential that your dog pairs your words with her actions. This means she has to hear them, and they have to be said at the right moment. This is crucial. Project your voice a little and call her name as you would when she's 50 yards away from you in the park. That's the sound you want to associate with the head-snap! And she doesn't get a treat till you've said "Yes".

I'm getting bored.

If *you're* getting bored, what hope is there for your dog? Maybe you're going on too long. Your training sessions need only be very short - one minute to start with, three minutes at the outside - and enthralling. Five treats may be enough for some dogs. Stop while you're ahead. You want your dog's reaction at the end of a training session to be "Really? I was enjoying that!" rather than "At last. Thank goodness that's over."

She's brilliant at this game at home in the kitchen but really distracted at the park.

Too soon! Too soon to be taking the game on the road. Don't fall into the trap of testing your dog. You need to focus on teaching, not testing. Are you perhaps a male? I find that it's a boy-thing to want to test and say, "What if…" While this may make you a great and intrepid explorer, it's not what we're looking for in the nursery! Don't unravel your work before it's firmly installed! We will be building up to adding distractions, once we know this Name Game is known and loved.

All this food! I expect my dog to come because I say so.

Then you'll get a slow and intermittent recall. Everyone on the planet is concerned with *What's in it for me?* Do you go to work? Do you get a pat on the head every Friday or do you expect your employer to pay you? If he said, "I expect you to work for me because I say so," would you be back on Monday?

My dog's doing fine then gets distracted by the children or a noise outside.

Well observed. If your dog is distracted, make some attractive kissy noises to get her focus back. Don't use her name unless you can put money on her coming back to you (remember Rule 3 in the last section of Chapter 2: *Only call your dog when you have a 90% chance of her coming*). As soon as she turns and looks at you it's "Yes!" and you're back in the game. Just pick up your rhythm again from there. Having your dog focus on you when there are distractions is exactly what we're building towards.

She can do this. What next?

That's great! We will be extending this game and moving towards a real-life outdoor recall, but this is a game my own dogs love to play at any stage in their life. It's always building a firm base for your recall. So keep playing the game. We'll move in baby steps towards the perfect recall. Don't push the scaffolding away too soon!

What do I do if she wanders off?

The first thing to do is examine what *you're* doing. Try videoing with your smartphone - it may reveal you to be uninteresting and static or you may pick up the moment when your dog switches off. Is it something you said? I'd make attractive sounds - cooing or clucking, but not saying her name - to regain her focus, then tell her, "Oh dear, you missed a treat," pause for effect, then start the game again. This game is undemanding and enjoyable - don't overcomplicate it!

Taking the Name Game on the road

Once you're getting a fast and eager response indoors, you can start venturing outside with the Focus Game. You'll move on to the Name Game when you're getting the same speed, enthusiasm, and attention as you get inside.

1. Try the garden first. You need to find an area where your treats will be clearly visible. We don't want your dog to have to hunt for her rewards. Paving stones are good, or you can put down two towels or trays and buzz your treat onto them each time.

2. If your dog instantly goes mentally AWOL as soon as you go through the door, start working your way towards the open door while playing the game, until one treat is in the house and the other in the garden.

3. Remember to keep your sessions very short - two minutes max.

4. If your dog is going well and fast in the back garden, try the front of the house, perhaps your driveway or the pavement outside. Use a good length lead for this.

5. Take this gradually and always top up the enthusiasm by playing back in the house between times. Grab all those little opportunities the day presents to pick up half a dozen treats and spend them on a quick Name Game.

6. When this is all going well, you can try the park. Choose a time when it's fairly quiet, and you can find space away from everyone else to play your game. Use tree-stumps for your treats or place two towels down so she can find the rewards instantly.

Your aim is for your dog to respond automatically to her name, regardless of the distraction. Like teaching a child to swim, we only gradually move up towards the deep end of the pool as the child's confidence and ability grows. Keep to baby steps - stay in the shallow end! - but at the same time don't get bogged down and not move forward at all. The game needs to be edging forward a little all the time.

Watchpoints

If your dog has a history of running off, you may like to use a long line. To begin with you can hold the end, but as your dog becomes more invested in the game, you may let it trail on the ground. A line of 30 feet is a good length. It should be attached to the back clip of a harness rather than the collar. If you have to stamp on the line as it flies past you with a disappearing dog on the end, you don't want to put your dog in traction for a neck injury afterwards!

- If your dog is a new rescue dog and you don't know what to expect, use the long line for safety.
- Your dog may be fearful and tend to run away when panicked: use the long line.

When you play this game you are building in excitement and joy for your dog. There's no place for fierce name-calling, "Ah-ahs," "Nooooo," and the like. If you find yourself a bit gruff and short, then talk to your dog as if she's a toddler. Remember the Marshmallow Test - you must be consistent and reliable: she must know that responding to her name is always good.

Troubleshooting

My dog finds the grass fascinating and goes off sniffing.

Try and find a less exciting surface to play on. If your dog is sniffing before locating the treat, she may be missing your bowling action when you put the treat down. Go back to placing it with your hand and see if she gets it then. If she's taking the treat then wandering off, it may be that your treats are crumbly and encouraging her to hoover - or it may be that she finds the scents more stimulating than your game. Hmmm. Food for thought there! First, you should make your game and treats irresistible - and place them, clearly visible, on your flat surface. Second, go over and silently slip your hand in her collar, gently draw her back to where she got her treat. By now she'll be looking at you, so say, "Yes!" and bowl your next treat onto your stone or towel right next to your foot. Go back to getting the game enthusiastic indoors, then in your garden. Always aim to get a rhythm going.

In the park my dog seems very anxious about any other dogs or people. She's always been shy.

Give her some distance from the things she's worrying about. This will allow her to indulge in the game without anxiety. This game should be undiluted fun.

I've been to the park. Now what?

Go there again. Play this game daily. You want to practice some form of recall daily for ever more - even if it's only for three seconds. All my dogs get very excited when I start the Name Game with them!

In the park there are squirrels!

Squirrels are the top distraction for many dogs. Calling a dog off squirrels or rabbits takes time, but it is most certainly possible. We'll be going deeper into this in a later chapter - Chapter 5 "Taking it outside - Rabbits and other Beasts" But don't go there yet! There's so much more to learn first. For now, find a squirrel-free zone to practice. Perhaps the middle of a big field? The beach? Keep in mind that your greatest distractions will be turned to your advantage. More about that in the next Chapter!

My treats don't seem to be so attractive when we're out!

Good point: for the counter-attractions of the great outdoors you need the heavy artillery in your pocket! This leads us nicely to the next Chapter, where we'll be looking at all the things you can do to load the dice in your favour.

In this Chapter you've learnt:

- It's all games to them
- Fun is the quickest way to learn
- Dogs learn by rhythm and patterning
- "I love these bouncy games!"

Chapter 4
Four more classic recall games

Great recalls from pup and toddler!

So you and your dog are having a ball playing the games in Chapter 3: Now the Fun Starts! The games are fast, fun, and can occur at any moment in the day - not in special "training sessions." You should be getting that head snap now whenever you call your dog's name.

In this chapter, we will learn four more games designed to make the recall the high point of your dog's day. They all emphasise slightly different aspects. To start with, approach them in the order given here. in time you can mix and match. The fourth game is more challenging and will need to be taught carefully and without error, gradually increasing the level of difficulty.

First, we're going to take your head-turn further, getting a fast and furious game going! Instead of Name = Head-turn, we're now going to get Name = Head-turn and *run!*

Lesson 3: The Running Name Game

I'll explain this as simply as possible, but to help you get it going well, keep in mind your aim: Name = Head-turn and run.

1. Start your Focus Game.
2. As soon as you have a rhythm, move into your Name Game. Spend a few treats on establishing a rhythm here.
3. Now, as your dog dives for the treat and you say her name, you turn your body so you're facing away from her and run away. Keep looking over your shoulder so you can mark her head-turn with a "Yes!" as before. What's going to happen here is that as your dog turns, she'll see your backside departing - she'll run to catch up with you!
4. As she catches up, toss your treat ahead of both of you. As she dives for the treat, say her name, turn your body away from her in the other direction, watching over your shoulder so you can say, "Yes!" at the right moment. Again, throw your treat forward as she runs past you.

Get this rhythmic, fast - and fun! Play this game for a small handful of treats at least once a day, perhaps when you put the kettle on.

Troubleshooting

A snail would move faster than my dog.

You may need to run yourself to get her excited and moving. You may get away with just turning and taking a step or two away. If your dog is very small, you can run in little steps so that it looks as though you're running fast - but you're not covering much ground. This game has to be fun and enticing! Check out the quality and desirability of your treats, and when your dog last ate or rested. Be incredibly exciting for just 60 seconds! Your game should be more fun than a squirrel skittering up a tree.

She's bouncing beside me trying to snatch the treat from my hand.

Remember to keep your hands out of the way. You're not holding the treat out to her are you? *Are you?* She only gets the treat thrown as a reward for turning and racing to you. No waving the treat about to tempt her!

I'm hopeless at this - I can't dance either.

Perhaps you can use the pattern on your flooring, or the lines of the floorboards to guide you. We don't want you crashing into the wall! Line yourself up between two markers - the cupboard and the window, perhaps. You'll be turning to face the cupboard, calling your dog and turning to face the window. You need only move very little - it's the dog that's doing the running. Be enthusiastic and get her excited!

Going sideways has me tripping over.

Don't go sideways! Turn so your bum is towards your dog. The fact that you appear to be leaving will make her run faster. If you're going sideways, it's a pretty good bet you're waving your treat about at arms' length too. Turn completely away from your dog, watch over your shoulder to mark her head-turn, and keep your hands and treats to yourself.

I'm puffed out from all this running!

Make sure you're only doing a couple of steps - just enough to get your dog running - before you toss your treat and turn. Your dog should always be covering much more ground than you. Once you get a rhythm going you may just need to spin your body as if leaving to get your dog racing! *Never run ahead of your dog.*

Saying her name seems to make her slow down.

Call her name, joyfully, as you would if she were 50 yards way in a field. There's no room for a stern voice. Imagine you're calling a small child. Some people can sound a bit menacing when they say the name flatly and without enthusiasm. If you're male, you may need to go up an octave! Call excitedly! This will have her racing, tail a-wag.

Lesson 4: Puppy Pingpong

This is a great game, adored by my crew, who love to run great distances while playing it. That will come later - for now you'll be starting with - you guessed it! - a very short distance. You want your dog to have success from the start.

You need two or more people to play this game. Children love it, so you may be able to get some peace and quiet from the kids and the dog for a couple of minutes! Of course, you need to teach the children first and supervise till you know they have the game down without fighting and confusing the dog.

1. Start with two people facing each other, about four yards apart. Both people should have a handful of yummy treats.

2. Person A calls the dog *without using her name.* The reason why will become clear when you start the game. So you can call - excitedly, of course! - "Doggiedoggiedoggie!" "Here pup!" "Woo-woo-woo!" – whatever gets your dog into the game. Do *not* wave your treat about for inspection! Keep your hands to yourself. You're not luring an action: you're going to reward your dog's good choice.

3. As she runs towards Person A, he places a treat between his (own) feet. This means the dog has to run right up to the person, and not run past, run round, or - worst of all - hang about just out of arm's reach! It also means Person A won't be getting two paws amidships as the dog thunders in to him and leaps up for a reward.

4. Just as your dog is zeroing in on the treat, Person B calls her *not using her name* - "Doggiedoggiedoggie!" or whatever works for you. Now your dog has to leave someone she knows has food, to go to the person who's calling her and may not have anything. If she gets stuck staring adoringly at Person A, that person should look away, be boring, and totally ignore the dog. Person B, on the other hand, is dancing a jig and hooting happily - see why children have fun with this game? You need to play uninhibitedly! At last she'll turn and head towards Person B who will reward between his feet as before.

5. Once your dog gets the hang of this, she'll start to race between the two of you, pausing only to snatch the treat between the feet and spin back. This is excellent!

6. Now you can add her name as she's turning and running towards you. You are labelling her action of rushing towards you as "Ditzy!" - this will come to mean "run with joy and enthusiasm towards me!"

Troubleshooting

I've got a big dog. She doesn't get up much speed over four yards.

Very true: a big dog needs a larger turning circle, so as soon as you've got a rhythm going, you can take a step backwards each time your dog is heading away from you. Gradually you'll extend the distance till your dog can turn comfortably and run really fast between you - but it's important that you both start close to ensure the dog gets the game.

My puppy is small - she's getting worn out!

That sounds good! What's better than a tired and happy dog who is learning a cracking fast recall? Keep the distance between you short and the sessions equally short, just a couple of minutes. Remember to stop while she's still enthusiastic.

When I call she comes quickly, but when my husband calls she wanders slowly to him.

There can be a number of reasons for this. Women are most often the nurturers, so from the moment your puppy's eyes were open she's probably been used to females. Maybe also you are the principal carer at home, so she's not so familiar with your husband. Another thing may be that men can move more stiffly, heavily, and menacingly than women and their voices may be more suited to the boardroom or the parade ground than the nursery. Get your husband to access his inner girl and lighten up! A relaxed posture with light-hearted voice will make a big difference. He may have to make his voice higher - like when calling a small child.

When can we play this in the park?

Good question! Once you are all happy and confident in this game, and your dog is responding to her name, you can start in the park. If it's a busy day with lots of dogs and children running about, get as far as you can from the action and work the game over a very short distance. This will give your dog the best chance to succeed. If it's quiet, then you can start with a longer distance between you because there are no distractions. Always aim for success.

Where else could we play Puppy Pingpong?

If you're struggling to make time for your games - although it's only a minute or so at a time - remember a good way to play Puppy Pingpong is when one of you is slaving over a hot stove in the kitchen and the other is sitting with feet up in front of the television in the living room. (Which way round this is in your household is entirely up to you!) You'll know when to call your dog as you'll hear your partner's joyous exclamation when she arrives for her treat, so call right away. Depending on the size and layout of your house, this could be quite a long distance agility course! If there's a slippery floor where your dog needs to corner, put down a mat so that she doesn't skid and injure herself. Once you've got this working in the house, you can try with one of you in the house and the other in the garden - have fun with this!

Lesson 5: Cannonball Recall

Bella explodes forward when called

The key to a fast recall is a fast start. We've been working on that instant head-snap when your dog hears her wonderful name. So far all the games have focussed on this skill. Now, we want to go for an explosive release from whatever she's doing when you call her! If the cannonball is launched without much power, it'll dribble out of the cannon and thud to the ground. Put plenty of gunpowder behind it and it will shoot out - unstoppable - till it hits its target. When you call your dog in this game, she will burst forward with such energy that she's nearly reached you before she's started! What better - and more enjoyable - way to practice that fast recall?

Like Puppy Pingpong, you need two people for the Cannonball Recall.

1. Person A holds the dog loosely around the shoulders and chest - not by the collar or harness.

2. Person B takes a couple of steps away from the dog, maybe three or four yards at most. Turn slightly away from your dog and start to bounce excitedly to wind her up. Call out anything but her name: "Ready! Steady! Readyreadyready!"

3. Once she's looking ready to burst, Person B calls her name and starts to run away. *At the same moment* Person A, the holder, lets go of the dog.

4. She will shoot forward as though shot from a cannon. Person B is by now racing away with dog in hot pursuit.

5. When your dog catches up, reward her with a treat, a game with a toy, or even rolling on the ground with her!

This game always results in laughter and joy all round!

Two brothers play the Cannonball Recall with their puppy Cai

Troubleshooting

My dog backs out of the holder's embrace and bursts forward before I'm ready to call her.

That sounds like a good problem to have! Either the dog is not happy with the person who's holding her or she's desperate to get to you. Try and get your name call to coincide with her moment of escape - then run.

If I call and the holder doesn't let go, she won't come at all.

It's the caller (Person B) who decides when the dog is ready to explode forward. The holder only has to let go as soon as he hears the dog's name. Try not to miss the moment or your dog will get confused. You will actually be teaching her *not* to come when she's called. Oops.

I really can't run very well and definitely not fast.

That's ok. Once you've got the game going and understood, you can start a bit further out from your dog so you're getting a head start. When she starts towards you, turn and run on the spot pumping your elbows, in slow motion if necessary, so that it looks as though you're getting away. This game is a "Chase and Running Reward" game (see Chapter 1 on instinctive drives: *"Control the rewards and you control the dog"*). It adds urgency to your dog's response. You want the sound of your dog's name to elicit a head-snap turn, followed by an explosive bound and then a race to catch you up. If you can establish this, you'll find that when you call, your dog is halfway back to you without realising what's happening!

My dog is too excited to take the treat!

It sounds as if you're playing the game with huge enthusiasm, and his reward is chasing, catching, or overtaking you. This is brilliant, but you do need your dog to stop when he joins you. Maybe a favourite toy for him to latch on to?

I have to waggle the toy or treat around in my hand to get her to focus on me before I call her.

Don't let your dog decide whether or not she's going to come to you! If you show her the reward first, you give her the option of saying, "Nah, don't think I'll bother." Start much closer, sound much more exciting, and look much more active. Do very short, very quick Cannonball Recalls - perhaps as close as two yards - till she's got the idea.

My dog comes alright, but it's not what you'd call fast.

If your dog is a large and heavy breed, old, infirm, or overweight, you can't expect huge speed. What speed does he take off at when he sees a squirrel? A cat? Hears his dinner bowl clattering? That's the speed you want for your recall - always. You need to inject excitement into this chase game! Bounce on the spot and try calling as if the house is on fire - "ROVER!!!!!!!!!" This is no time for a subdued genteel voice.

Lesson 6: Torpedo Recall

Foodie-dog Lacy races towards me, flying by her bowl of food

Now you've got your dog spinning round when she hears her name. She's bursting to get to you, and she flies as fast as she can to catch up with you. We're going to add a bit of real life to the mix in the form of distraction. While the Cannonball Recall focusses on an explosive response, the Torpedo Recall is about your dog taking a straight line to you, without deviation!

To play the Torpedo Recall game, you need to know exactly how attractive various distractions are to your dog. You can list them and number them so that your dog's top distraction is something you'll gradually work up to.

For one of my dogs - Coco - any person or child within sight is a big distraction. If a person is walking towards us saying, "Hello," and gesturing excitedly, we are at Number One on Coco's personal distraction list: he's desperate to meet them and wiggle about at their feet.

For another of my dogs - Lacylu - food is a major distraction.

For Rollo the Border Collie it's seeing anything move: a broom sweeping, flies buzzing, a ball being thrown, and people running.

For Cricket the Whippet it's the tiniest movement in the undergrowth which suggests - bunnies!

You can see there's quite a list of major distractions in my household! Hence my head tends to spin on dog walks like a radar scanner checking out the distractions before they cause a problem. Make your own individual list, and we'll gradually inoculate your dog against the things that currently completely derail her brain.

Just a note: If your dog will stay where you put her for a moment you can play this game solo. Otherwise you'll need a helper to gently hold her till you're ready.

1. Practice a couple of straightforward, joyous, recalls as a warm-up.

2. Now take a very watered-down version of your dog's distraction, perhaps Number Ten on your list. For Coco this could be a person standing still, facing away, at a distance. For Lacylu, it's an empty food packet or bowl. Rollo's sheepdog eye will be caught by anything that may move fast, so just a ball lying on the ground would be enough of a challenge for him. Cricket the bunny-hunter could be 100 yards from the nearest hedge or tree.

3. Make a triangular pattern with your dog on one corner, you on another corner, and the distraction at the third point. *This is not an equilateral triangle!* You could be 5 yards from your dog, and the distraction could be 50 yards away.

4. Call your dog to you and reward with enthusiasm with a treat or game, *then race together* to the distraction which she ignored, letting her interact with it: let social butterfly greet the person; give foodie dog another treat as if from the packet on the ground; throw the ball; allow rabbity dog a moment of snuffling in the undergrowth.

5. Repeat, with the distraction a little nearer.

6. Repeat, with it even closer.

7. Keep going till your dog has to swerve round the distraction to reach you. This may take you a month of practice! Don't make it too hard too soon!

Troubleshooting

I park my dog with a "holder" and walk away, but she only has eyes for the food bowl miles away.

You've clearly chosen the right distraction! She needs to be focussed at least partially on you before you call. Engage your dog before you leave her - dance about, move only a couple of yards away, then - while she's still looking at you - call excitedly, turn, and run. Your triangle may become a very weird shape, with you calling her and running in the opposite direction from the distraction. You can leave the food bowl empty, then fling a treat in as you both get there after your recall. That way, if she should make a mistake, she'll find a disappointingly empty bowl. The only way the bowl will "pay" is by getting there via you.

As soon as I call her, and my friend lets go, my dog races straight to the distraction.

The distraction is too close, and you're not getting your pup's attention before you call. You can put the distraction further away - or position it behind your friend who's holding the dog - and you stay very close to call her to you. When she's reached you and claimed her reward, you can then shoot off with her to the distraction. You don't want your dog claiming the prize without permission. So if it's a food bowl distraction, the bowl is empty till you get there with the food; if it's a toy distraction, try hanging it over a high branch so she can't get it till you're there; if it's a person distraction, the person can refuse to interact with the dog unless you arrive with her.

My dog's bonkers. She can't sit still for me to call her.

Try with a friend holding her, like for the Cannonball Recall. Be as quick as you can setting her up, leaving, then calling. You can stretch out the time between leaving her and calling her once she's got the idea. Don't forget to race with enthusiasm to the distraction once she's arrived with you.

My dog doesn't pay attention till I've called her several times.

Remember "Call just once" from Chapter 2? Each time you repeat the call you are hammering another nail into the coffin of your recall. You are teaching your dog to ignore you until you stop. Call just once - excitedly. If she doesn't respond you can go back to her and re-set her. Keep her focus from the moment the game begins, and always move fast!

My dog comes straight to me brilliantly, but then she beats me to the distraction.

This is excellent enthusiasm and you've clearly chosen a great reward for her. Catch her collar when she arrives with you or leave a lead trailing from her collar for you to catch up. Now you can run *together* to her reward.

My dog doesn't even notice the distraction.

Either your distraction isn't hitting the spot or it's too far away. You can approach the bowl/toy/person yourself before you call her, to draw her attention to it. Then run back to her, step away a couple of yards and call.

My dog started out well, but after a while she gets bored.

Boredom is the antithesis of fun training! As soon as she's played the game well a couple of times, move on to something else. Also, be sure that the distraction really is her favourite thing on earth. If she's a foodie dog and she gets a tasty morsel thrown in the bowl when you both race towards it, why would she be bored?

I'm not getting enthusiasm.

Then I think your dog may be a little confused. You haven't been telling her off, have you? This may have the effect of rooting her to the spot, unsure of what she's meant to do. Make it crystal clear, aim for success - even if your distraction has to be almost in the next parish to begin with - and only gradually make it harder. You would do well to go back to the Running Name Game to rebuild her confidence that she can do it right.

Distractions and Distance

Not a game, but two very important Ds to incorporate into your training as you go. The key is to only ever add one at a time. So if you're in the park and it's nice and quiet, try calling your dog from a good distance, then from a shorter distance, then perhaps from a greater distance. If the park is busy and full of activity, then it's a time for very short recalls.

Don't ask too much at once! Remember you're always aiming for success - you're teaching, not testing.

In this chapter we've learnt:

- Making everything a game is the quickest way for your dog to learn
- Four great recall games
- "Pavlov is on your shoulder" - get a knee-jerk reaction to your call
- "When I'm called I get the opportunity to run as fast as I can!"

Chapter 5
Taking it outside - rabbits and other beasts

What's caught Saxon's eye?

As detailed in Chapter 1 *"Control the rewards and you control the dog"*, you need to work against your dog's biggest distractions, and where possible, make them a reward. Some distractions, clearly, cannot be offered as a reward!

When I'm in a safe place - where I'm familiar with the terrain and the boundaries, and we're far from roads - and I have called Cricket the Whippet back from a rabbit hunt successfully a number of times, I'll tell her, "Off you go!" and release her as a reward. If she chooses to go and hunt rabbits that's fine, but most often she will start out, then decide that she'd rather stay with us. (She never actually catches one, you understand - it's just the fun of the hunt. I wouldn't use this as a reward if I had a chasing-killing dog.) You can adopt the same strategy with quite a few other rewards too.

- The children are playing ball in the garden, and your dog is desperate to join them. Call her to you, tell her how good she is - then let her out to join them.
- There are friendly dogs playing at the park while you're on a walk, and your dog hauls you along on the lead, trying to get to them. Call her once and make a huge fuss of her when she focusses on you. Then tell her "Go play!" and release her to play.
- Your dog is merrily digging a crater in your flowerbed. Call her, reward her warmly for coming to you, then run to the spot you have chosen for her to dig in - you can partially bury some plastic bottles and the like there, and encourage her to dig. This is a perfect reward for a digger.

As you can see, Impulse Control is a major factor in all these situations. You can learn all about impulse control in the second book in this series of Essential Skills,

Leave it! How to teach Amazing Impulse Control to your Brilliant Family Dog.

What you're doing in these games is giving the dog a choice. The right choice will earn her what she's telling you she wants - plus a treat or two and your pleasure. Choice is as important in a head-snapping recall as it is in the rest of your dog's life. What we're teaching here is for her always to make the right choice - and that is to come when called!

Those squirrels!

Remember if you don't want your dog to develop a habit, you mustn't let her practice doing it!

Practice makes perfect - whether it's something you want or something you don't want.

If every time you get to the park, your dog bolts to the trees to look for squirrels, don't watch her and complain she's at it again. This is reminiscent of Ditzy's owner, expecting - miraculously - a different outcome. Fetch her, take her gently away from the squirrelly area, and engage her with a thrilling game of speed with you. You're not speedy? That's ok - just learn how to throw a frisbee and teach her how to catch!

Working your recall to the level that allows you to call your dog away from her greatest fixation will take time. This is why you want to start simply and work up. And it's why you want to get your games "classically conditioned" - an automatic response. Just like Pavlov's dogs licking their lips in anticipation of food when the bell was rung, your dog's name should have the same visceral effect. When I called people-crazy Coco the other day, in full flight towards a walker, his reaction was dramatic. It was as if the power drained out of his legs for a moment, as he stopped suddenly, turned, and whizzed back to me at high speed. He didn't have to think about this - it just happened. He's probably still wondering how!

Perhaps your dog is mad for squirrels? Try a squirrel-free area for your walks - perhaps the beach or the middle of a field? - and have her on a lead or long line attached to her harness when you have to be in Squirrelville. You'll be able to practise your recalls in the squirrel-free zone, and gradually you will be able to call her back on your walks through the forests too.

Don't expect too much too soon, Softly, softly, catchee monkey. This is a gradual process of repeatedly getting it right. With practice and consistency it will become automatic. If it all goes wrong, don't throw your hands in the air and give up! You just need to go back a step or two and reinforce what you've already taught, showing your dog that you expect the same response in any situation.

Recall training - like all dog training, really - goes on for the whole of the dog's life. You don't go to those six puppy classes and stop training! The intensive training will ease off, but refresher courses are always good. Spontaneous daily training, interspersed with your normal life, should become automatic. At what age do you stop helping and advising your children to make the best of their life? 6? 19? 32? Never? So it is with our dogs. We want them to have the best, most enjoyable, and freest life possible. We never stop interacting with them. We never stop teaching them.

In this Chapter you've learnt:

- The magic of the right and well-timed reward
- Knowing what your dog thinks is a reward
- Using a distraction as a reward
- "I'm glad I can still dig when I want to."

Conclusion
The end of this road - but the beginning of your journey

If you've been working along as you read this book, you'll already have noticed a huge improvement in your dog's recall! Congratulations! Now you see how well it works, you just have to keep it going - regularly.

You are now able to look forward to walks without stress and without the danger of your dog landing in all kinds of trouble. You are no longer shouting, getting cross, and asking yourself, "Whose idea was it to get a dog?" Even Ditzy and her owner will be able to go for a nice, pleasurable walk once they've worked through this book!

You'll be building gradually, keeping in mind that you're going through a complete re-training phase with older puppies and dogs - and rescue dogs who have entered your life with history. If you're lucky enough to be starting this with your brand-new puppy you'll never have to re-train! You'll have it right from the start.

So while this is going to be the new habit, give your dog time to remember each time what she's meant to do. Keep those rewards flowing freely whenever she does something you like!

Recalls and related things

You may think that to get a sparkling recall, every time, you need to practice millions of recalls out in the big wild world. You're partly right.

You do need to practice lots of recalls when your dog is in an excited state. It's no use having a perfect recall when there's absolutely nothing else for your dog to do! As you've seen, the foundations need to be laid in a distraction-free area - such as your home first - and gradually introduced to the wild. As you learn together, there are other experiences which may at first appear unrelated, but those experiences are actually a great help in the formation of your brilliant, fast, recall.

Reading the four books in this series of Essential Skills for a Brilliant Family Dog - and following the guidance *and* doing the work! - will give you everything you need for *your* Brilliant Family Dog! Once you have these four key pieces in place everything else will follow naturally. You will have built such value for what you do and what you want that your dog will happily learn, all her life. Once you have studied your dog and you know what is rewarding to her, you have the key to her heart.

Book 1. Calm Down! Step-by-Step to a Calm, Relaxed, and Brilliant Family Dog

Take a look at the first book in this series, *Calm Down! Step-by-Step to a Calm, Relaxed, and Brilliant Family Dog.* There you'll discover how to teach your dog to settle on a mat in a relaxed state - an off-switch for your dog! You'll also find out how to teach your dog when she may come off her mat, so she doesn't just wander off when she feels like it.

A mat is amazingly useful for your recall! You'll be able to park your dog without a helper to hold her - then walk or run away and call her from ever-increasing distances. Now you have a whole new dimension to enhance your recall work.

Remember to keep your dog's focus when you leave her parked for a recall. If she's looking everywhere but at you - then that's probably where she'll head when she's released! So be sure she remembers where she should be focussed while you depart.

And be sure to keep your different exercises "clean." If you take the mat outside and get poor matwork - not the sparkling attention and accuracy you've trained indoors - then stop mixing it up with anything else and go back to basics to re-establish the foundation skills. If you mix a poorly-executed game with a good one, you're more likely to spoil the good game than improve the poor one! It's all about the dog's attitude. If it's sloppy in one, then she'll think it's ok to be sloppy in the other.

It's ok! You'll get there, but observe what's happening on the way and never be afraid to go "backwards" in order to accelerate forwards.

Book 2. Leave it! How to teach Amazing Impulse Control to your Brilliant Family Dog

Here's another huge helper - and, of course, not just for recalls. Let this permeate all of your daily life with your dog, so she learns to think before she acts; she learns that all her actions have a consequence - some better than others; and she learns that she can earn greater freedom by exerting self-control. With proper impulse control, she won't have to be put away when you're eating or when visitors come, for instance, or kept on the lead all the time.

You'll be glad to know that there is a whole book devoted to this amazing and essential skill: *Leave it! How to teach Amazing Impulse Control to your Brilliant Family Dog*. In this book you'll learn how to amaze your friends with your dog's brilliant decisions. Just recently, Kelly told me proudly how she had taken her 15-week-old puppy Lottie to a pub lunch. Her family could not believe that Lottie was so well behaved! Lottie stayed on her mat the entire time, continually making good choices. She did not jump up, whine, nag, pester, steal food or any of the other things people might expect from such a young puppy.

Once your dog learns that it's all about choice - the choice she makes - you're halfway to training anything you want!

Book 3. Let's Go! Enjoy Companionable Walks with your Brilliant Family Dog

Why is walking nicely on the lead essential for your recall? It develops a mutual trust and tolerance between you and your dog which will spill over into all your life together. Reading *Let's Go! Enjoy Companionable Walks with your Brilliant Family Dog* will also teach you a whole lot about how force-free pro trainers use the lead to interact with their dog - and it's not by pulling or jerking it!

As with all these books, there are - sometimes surprising - parallels with working with your family and your colleagues. Learning Theory is not confined to quadrupeds, sea creatures, and birds - we humans are animals too, and we respond in exactly the same way!

It's a combination of the Recall games I've shown you here, and the Impulse Control you can learn from *Leave it! How to teach Amazing Impulse Control to your Brilliant Family Dog,* that allow me to call my Whippet, Cricket, off rabbits!

Whippets are the sprinters of the dog world - weight for weight, they are faster than both a racehorse and a greyhound, covering 200 yards in 12 seconds. That's a staggering 16 yards per second - 40 miles per hour. They are also bred specifically to catch hares and rabbits. You can see that if your recall is wobbly, then your Whippet could be under a car hundreds of yards away before you've got her name out of your mouth.

Resources

If you've got any specific queries, you can email me direct at beverley@brilliantfamilydog.com This will come straight to my personal inbox and I'll answer you - usually within 48 hours. Try me!

Meanwhile, for more free training, go to www.brilliantfamilydog.com and get a series of instructional emails on common day-to-day problems, like jumping up, chewing, barking, and so on.

> I am really enjoying your tips which you are sending me. *Maggie and Dottie*

> Many thanks for all your tips. They have really helped with my Jack Russell x Chihuahua puppy. *Melanie and Lola*

> I read your regular emails with interest having attended your puppy training sessions with our Shih Tzu Molly - she is a wonderful well-adapted dog who benefitted a lot (as did we!) from your training. *Una and Molly*

> I am very much enjoying and appreciating your emails. *Alex and her spaniel*

> Thank you for your recent emails and keeping us updated, and for sharing your easy to follow tips, helping us to help Smidge become our Brilliant Family Dog! *Janet and Smidge*

Works consulted for Chapter 2

http://www.nobelprize.org/nobel_prizes/medicine/laureates/1904/pavlov-bio.html accessed 2015

http://psychology.about.com/od/classicalconditioning/a/pavlovs-dogs.htm accessed 2015

Mischel, W., et al. (1989). *Delay of gratification in children.* Science, 24 4 (4907), 933–938

https://www.apa.org/helpcenter/willpower-gratification.pdf accessed 2015

Casey, B. J., et al. (2011). *Behavioral and neural correlates of delay of gratification 40 years later.* Proceedings of the National Academy of Sciences, 10 8 (36), 14998–15003

Harness

www.goodfordogs.co.uk/products for UK and Europe (see video)

I supply these harnesses to the British Isles and Europe. If you get one through me I will benefit financially - but it won't cost you any more. Watch the video. If you can find another harness that has the same effect, go for it!

http://2houndswholesale.com/Where-to-Buy.html for the rest of the world

Appreciation

I want to offer thanks to all those who have helped me get where I am with my dogs:

- First of all, my own long-suffering dogs! They have taught me so much when I've taken the time to listen.
- My students, who have shown me how they learn best, enabling me to give them what they need to know in a way that works for them.
- Some legendary teachers, principal amongst them: Sue Ailsby, Leslie McDevitt, Grisha Stewart, Susan Garrett. I wholeheartedly recommend them. They are trailblazers.

Free Training for you!

Jumping up?

Barking?

Chewing?

Get inventive solutions to everyday problems with your dog

www.brilliantfamilydog.com

About the author

I've been training dogs for many years. First for competitive dog sports and over time to be stellar family pets. For most of my life, I've lived with up to four dogs, so I'm well used to getting a multi-dog household to run smoothly. It soon became clear that a force-free approach was by far the most successful, effective, and rewarding for me and the dogs. I've done the necessary studying for my various qualifications - for rehab of anxious and fearful "aggressive" dogs, early puppy development, and learning theory and its practical applications. I am continually studying and learning this endlessly amazing subject!

There are some superb teachers and advocates of force-free dog training, and you'll find those I am particularly indebted to in the Resources Section. Some of the methods I show you are well-known in the force-free dog training community, while many have my own particular twist.

A lot of my learning has come through the Puppy Classes, Puppy Walks, and Starter Classes I teach. These dog-owners are not looking for competition-standard training; they just want a Brilliant Family Dog they can take anywhere. Working with real dogs and their real owners keeps me humble - and resourceful! It's no good being brilliant at training dogs if you can't convey this enthusiasm and knowledge to the person the dog has to live with. So I'm grateful for everything my students have taught me about how they learn best.

Beverley Courtney BA(Hons) CBATI CAP2 MAPDT(UK) PPG

Printed in Great Britain
by Amazon